BUSTY GIRL Comics

vol. 1

the first 100 comics from
Busty Girl Comics.com

by Paige "Rampaige" Halsey Warren

ISBN-13: 978-0615637259

If you would like to share the comics with friends and family, please either lend them your copy of this book or show them bustygirlcomics.com. Thanks for respecting me and my work. ♡

This book is dedicated
to my Mom, my Dad,
Cails, AJ, and Alex.

Seriously guys, I would not have been
able to create this webcomic and
subsequent book without your
constant support. ♡

Thanks for picking up this book!

I bet you didn't even come to this page first. I bet you just opened to somewhere in the middle of the book, read a comic cautiously to make sure it wasn't something dirty, and then proceeded to read the rest of the comics. It's cool. I do that too.

So, as you've realized by now, this is a comic about the perks and problems of being well-endowed in the chest area. If you ever feel encumbered by your breasts, whatever your measurements, then you're busty and I bet you'll relate to a bunch of these comics. And what if you don't consider yourself busty? Can you still read these comics?

. . . Yup! ☺ In fact, it's encouraged!

Now that I've got you hooked, you probably want more comics. Well, you're in luck! There's a new comic <u>every</u> <u>single</u> <u>day</u> over at BustyGirlComics.com and a whole network of busty recommendations, discussions, and advice too.

No, really, go check it out!

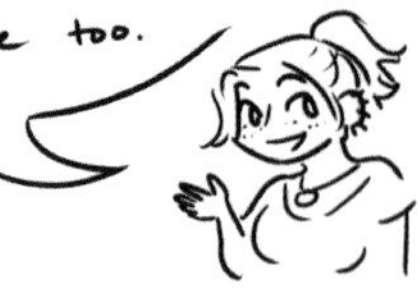

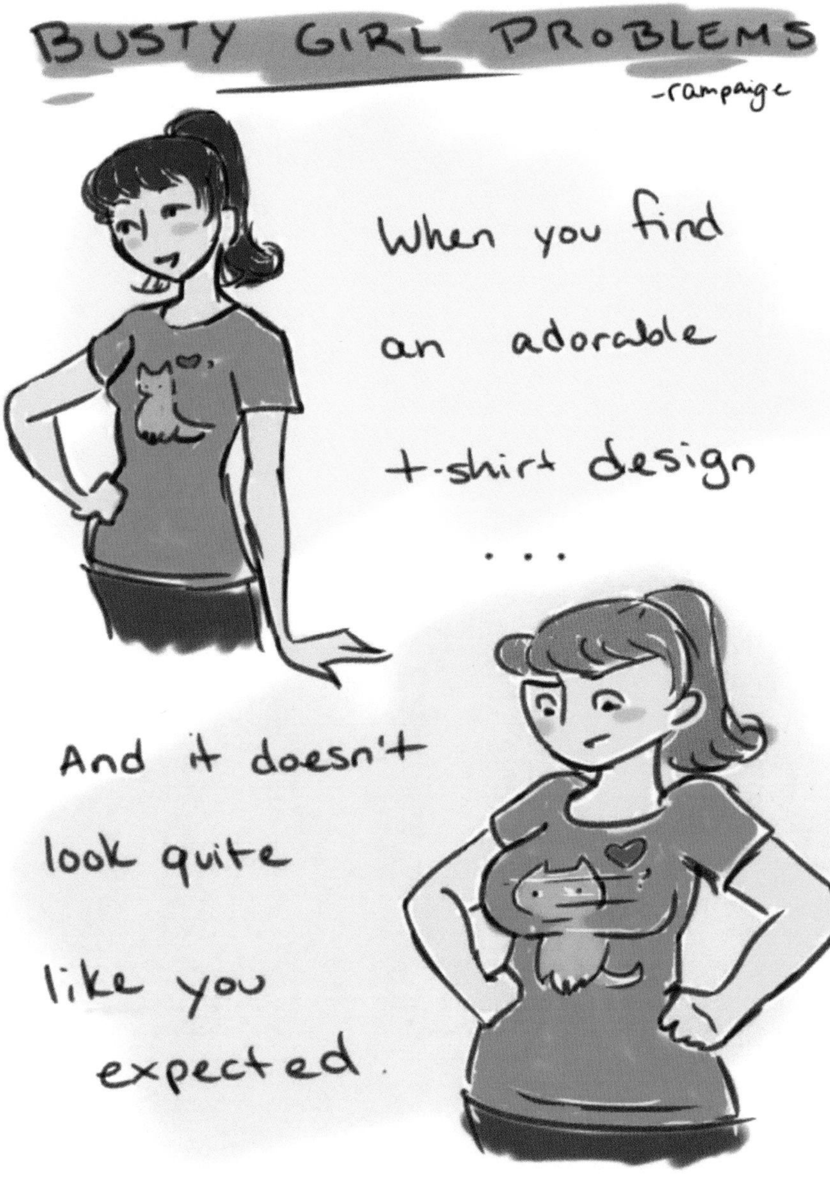
BUSTY GIRL PROBLEMS
-rampaige
When you find an adorable t-shirt design
. . .
And it doesn't look quite like you expected.

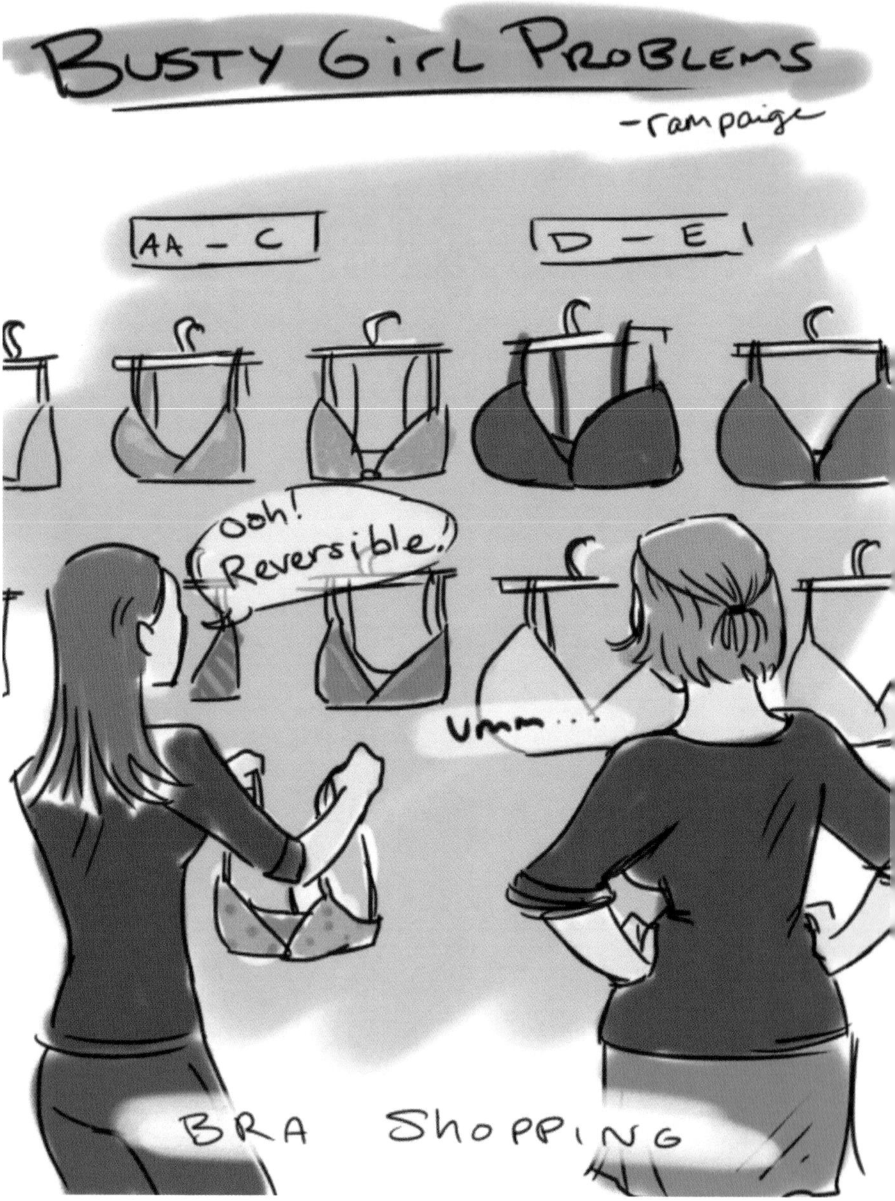
BUSTY GIRL PROBLEMS
-rampaige
AA - C
D - E
Ooh! Reversible!
Umm...
BRA SHOPPING

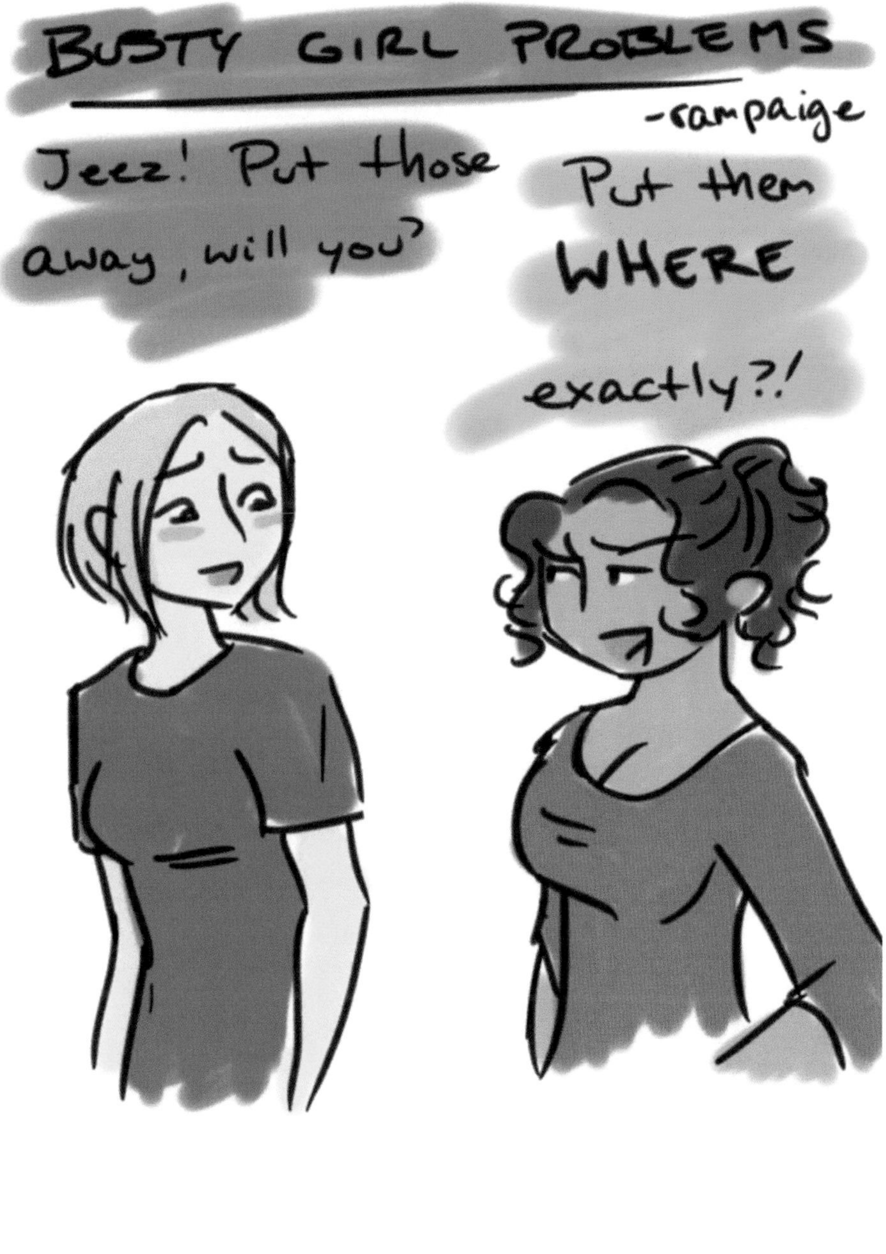
BUSTY GIRL PROBLEMS
-sampaige
Jeez! Put those away, will you?
Put them WHERE exactly?!

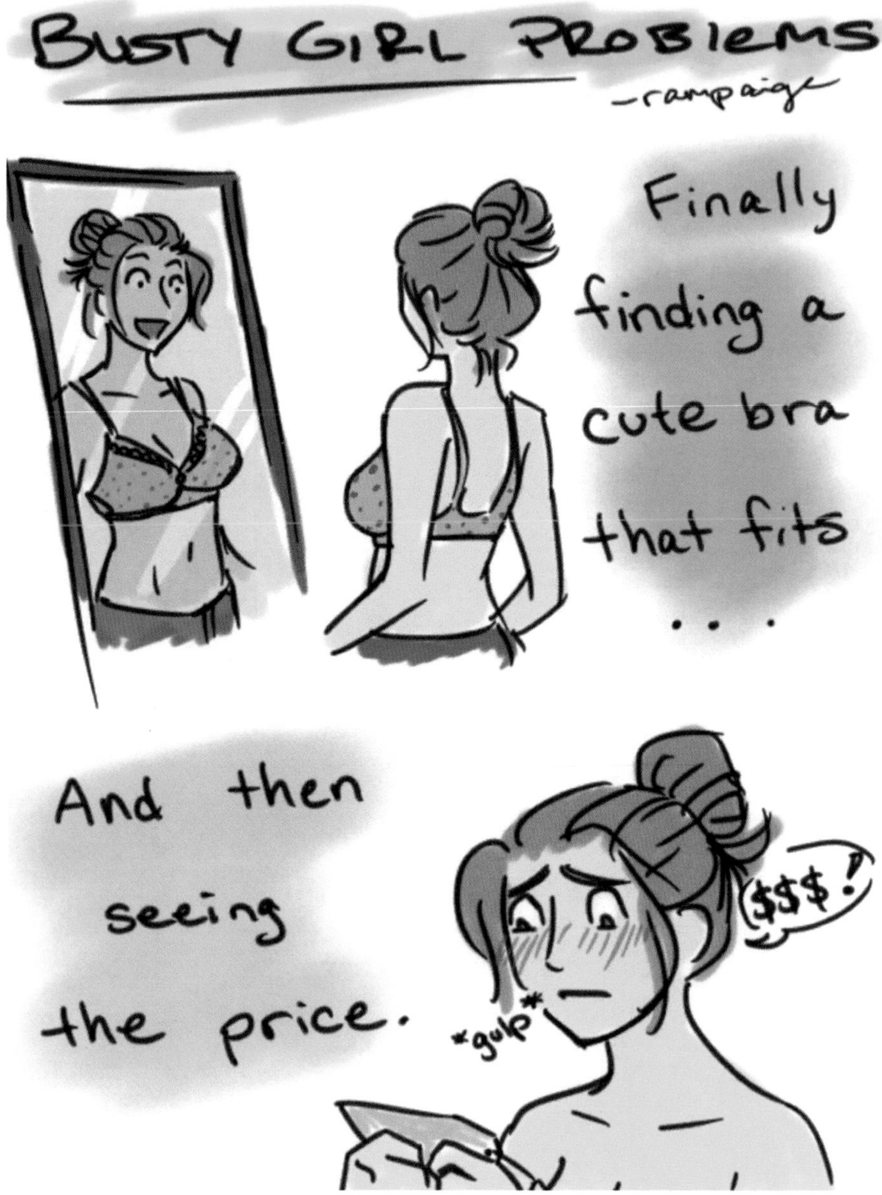
BUSTY GIRL PROBLEMS
-rampaige
Finally finding a cute bra that fits . . .
And then seeing the price.
gulp
$$$!

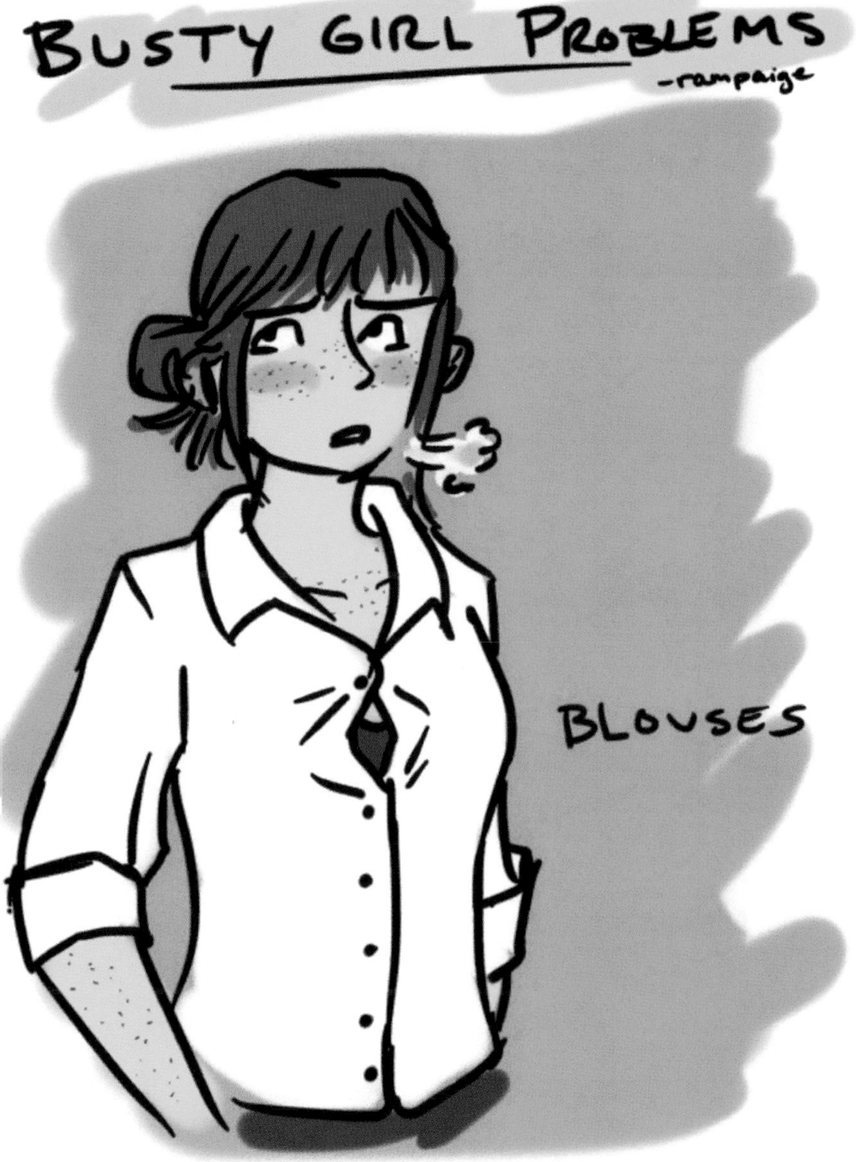
BUSTY GIRL PROBLEMS
-rampaige
BLOUSES

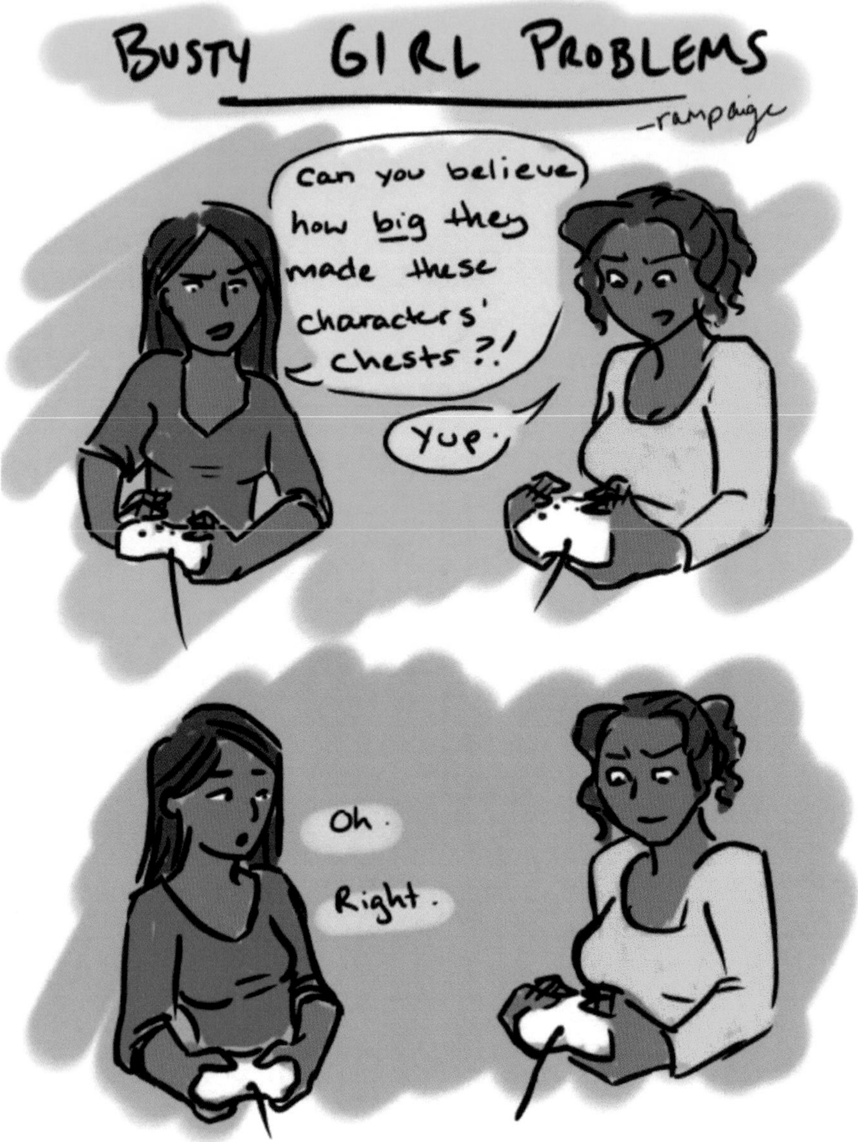
BUSTY GIRL PROBLEMS
-rampaige
Can you believe how big they made these characters' chests?!
Yup.
Oh.
Right.

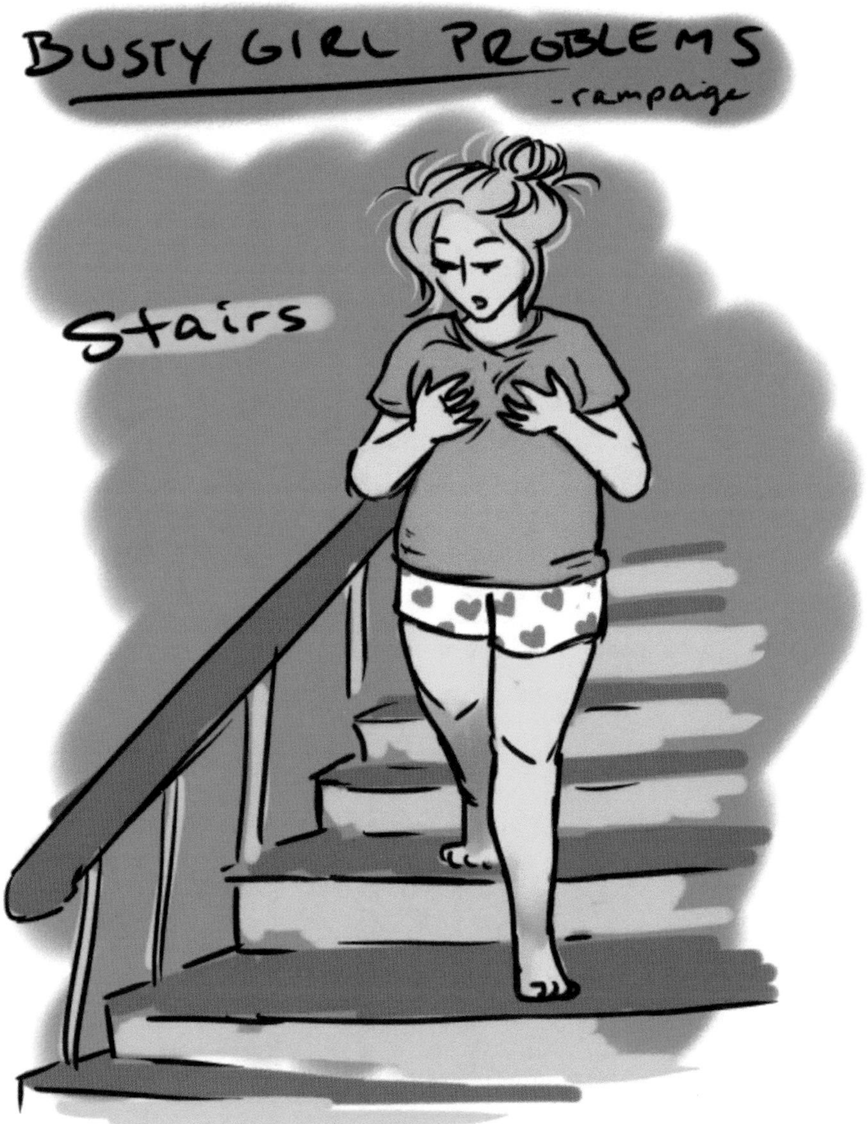
BUSTY GIRL PROBLEMS
-rampaige
Stairs

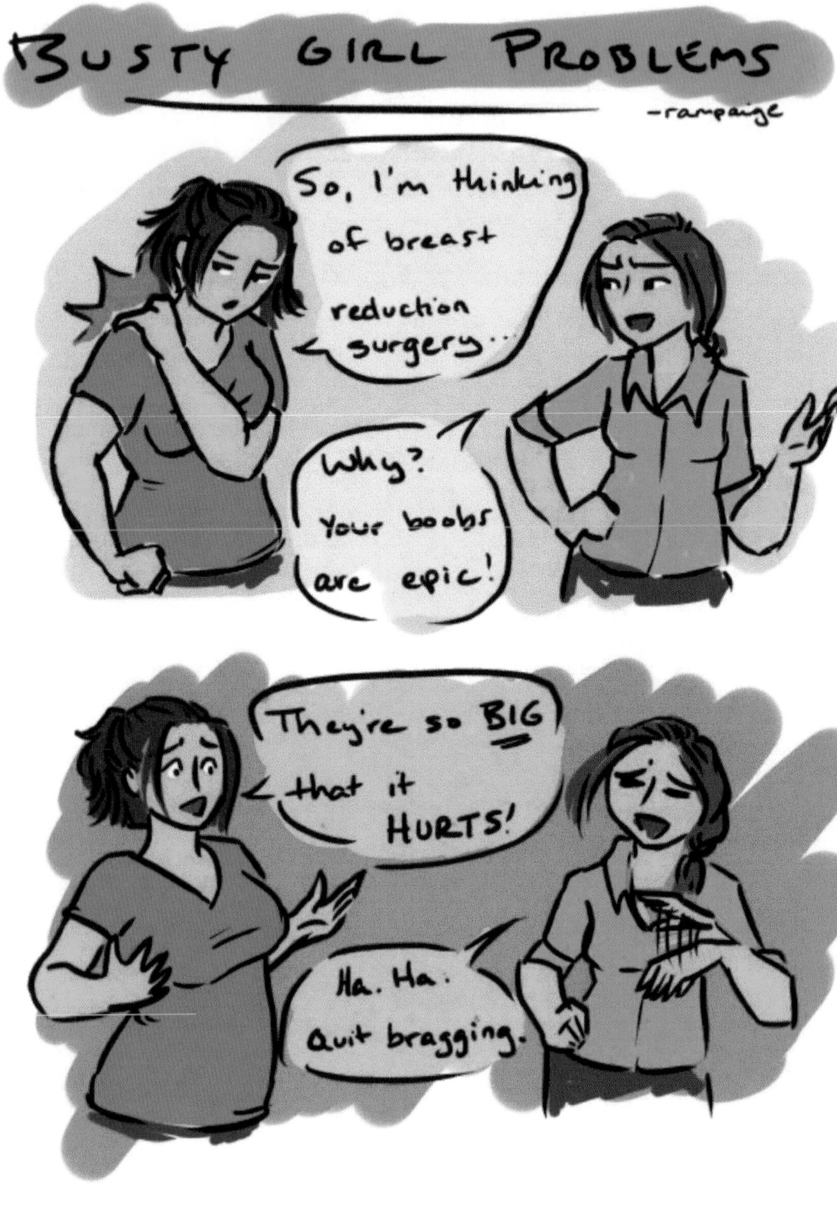
BUSTY GIRL PROBLEMS
-rampaige
So, I'm thinking of breast reduction surgery...
Why? Your boobs are epic!
They're so BIG that it HURTS!
Ha. Ha. Quit bragging.

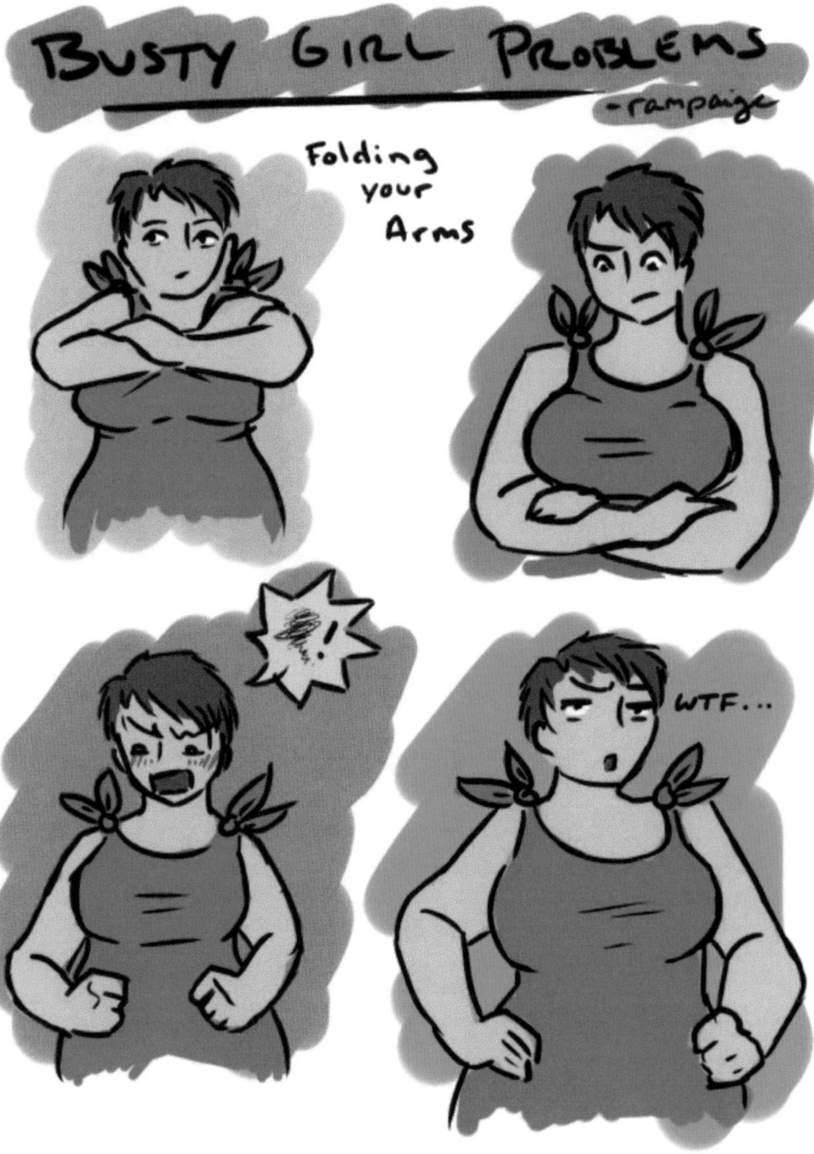
BUSTY GIRL PROBLEMS
-rampaige
Folding your Arms
!
WTF...

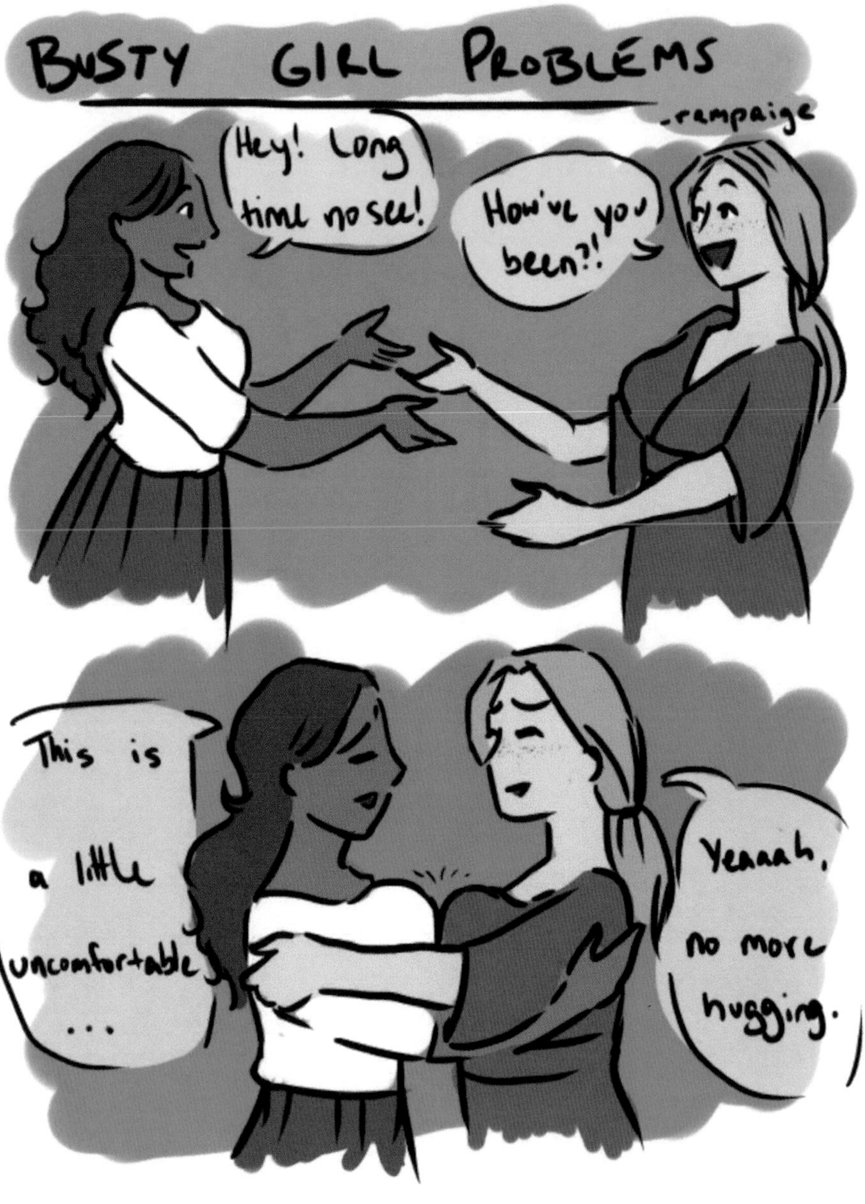
BUSTY GIRL PROBLEMS
-rampaige
Hey! Long time no see!
How've you been?!
This is a little uncomfortable...
Yeaaah, no more hugging.

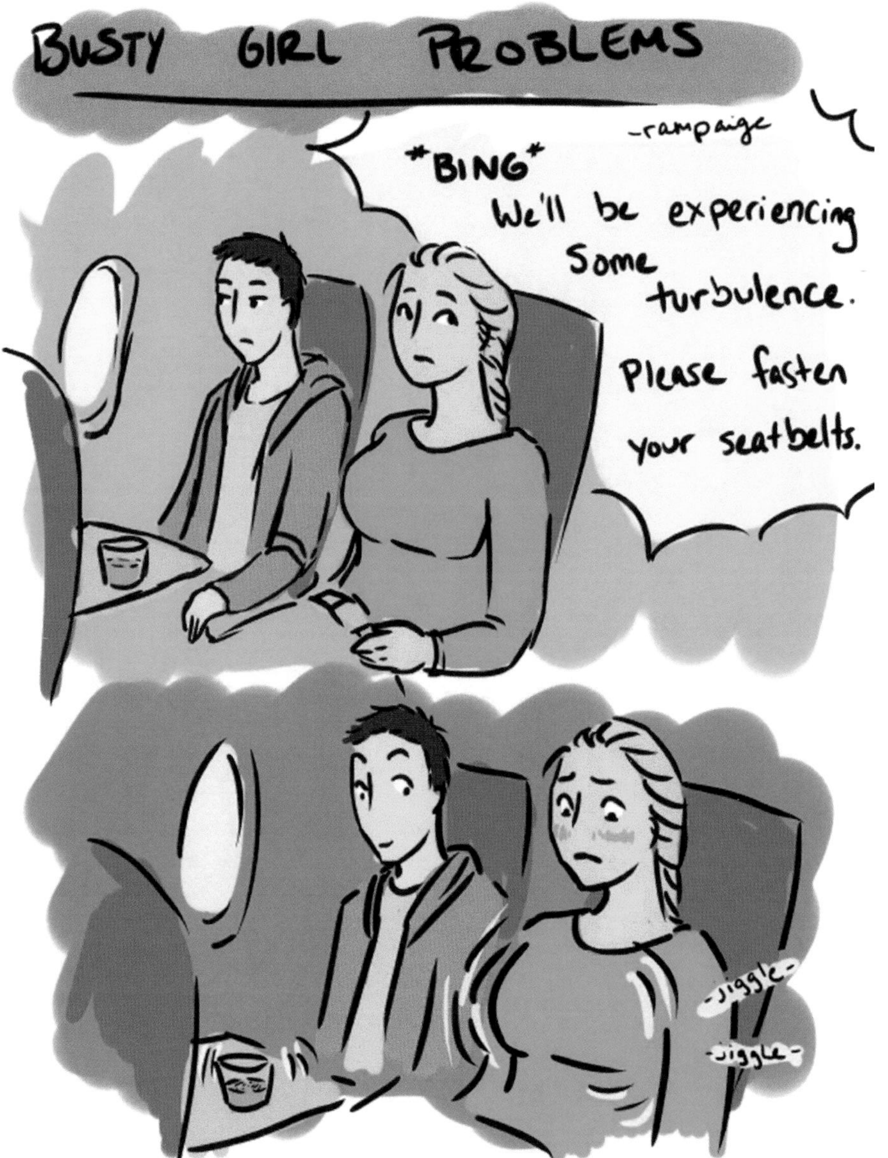
BUSTY GIRL PROBLEMS
-rampaige
BING
We'll be experiencing some turbulence.
Please fasten your seatbelts.
-jiggle-
-jiggle-

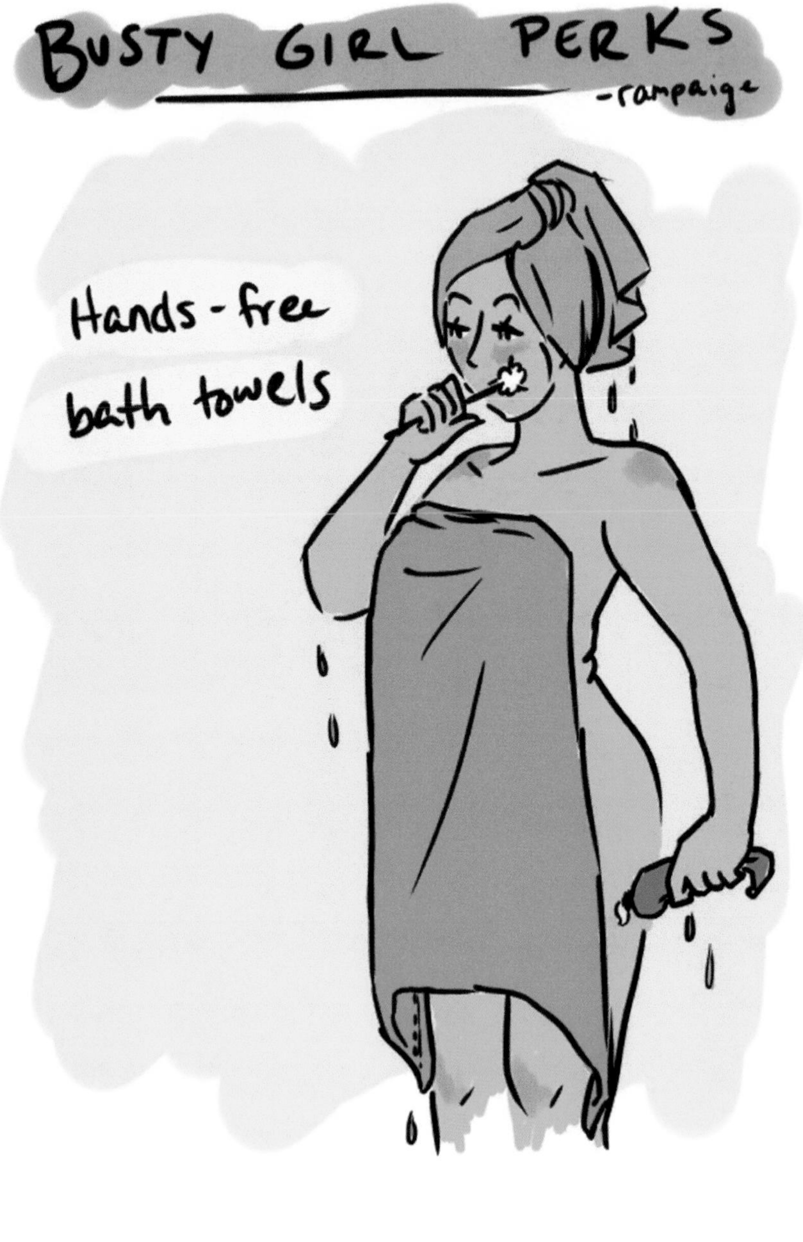
BUSTY GIRL PERKS
-rampaige
Hands-free bath towels

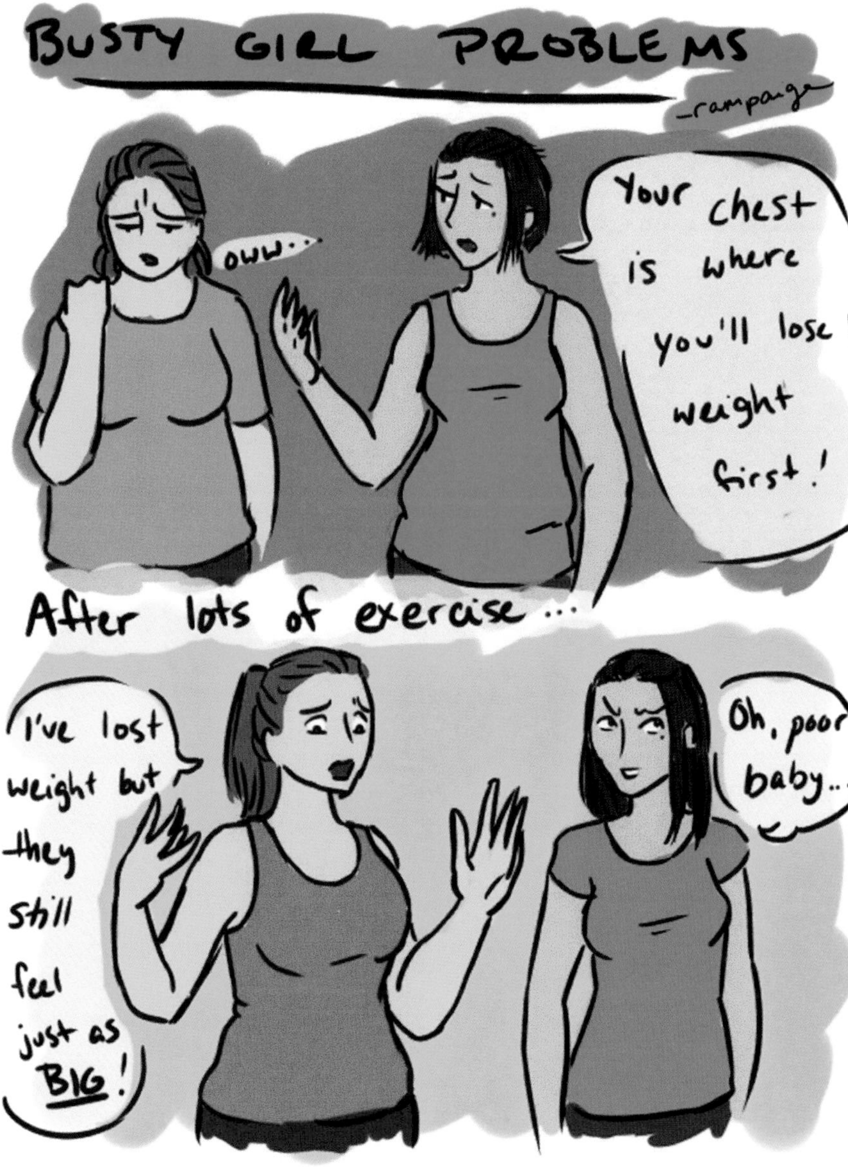
BUSTY GIRL PROBLEMS
-rampaige
oww...
Your chest is where you'll lose weight first!
After lots of exercise...
I've lost weight but they still feel just as BIG!
Oh, poor baby...

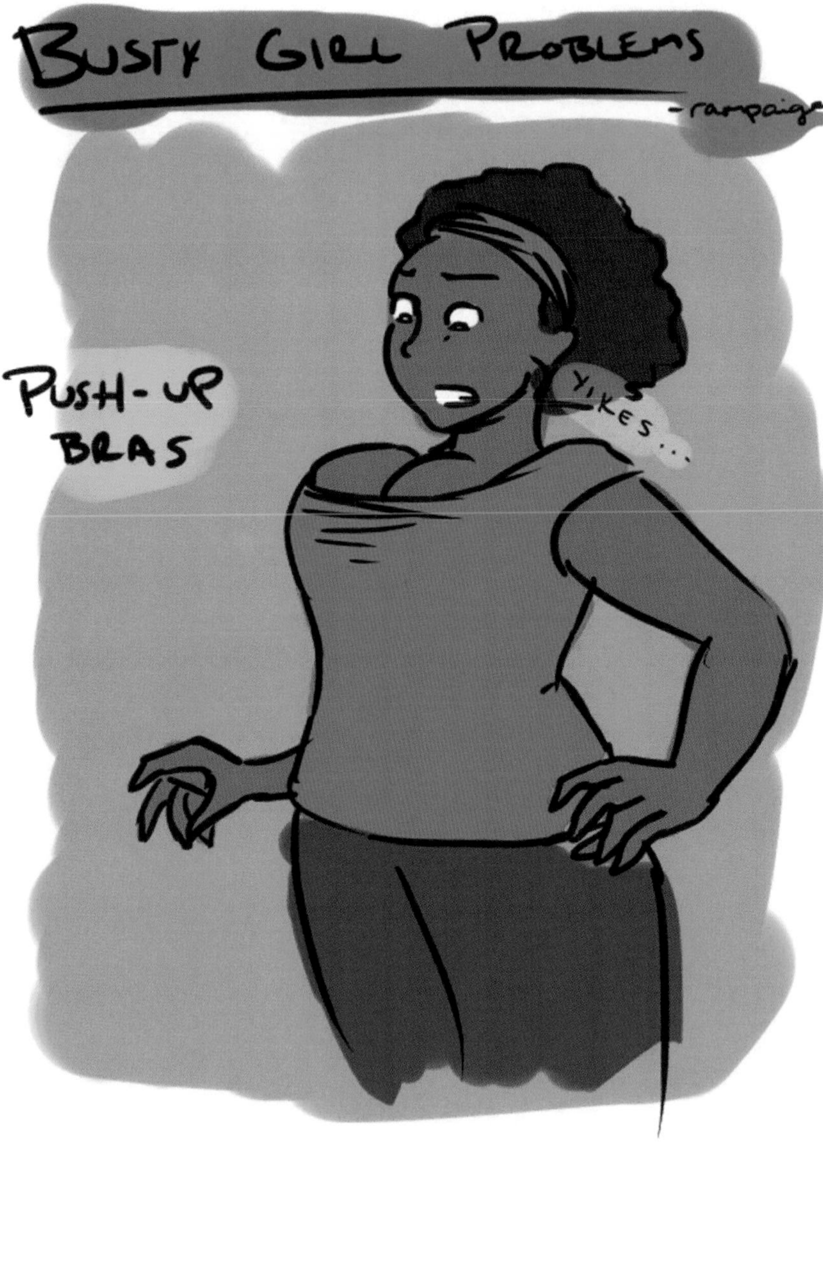
BUSTY GIRL PROBLEMS
-rampaige
PUSH-UP BRAS
YIKES...

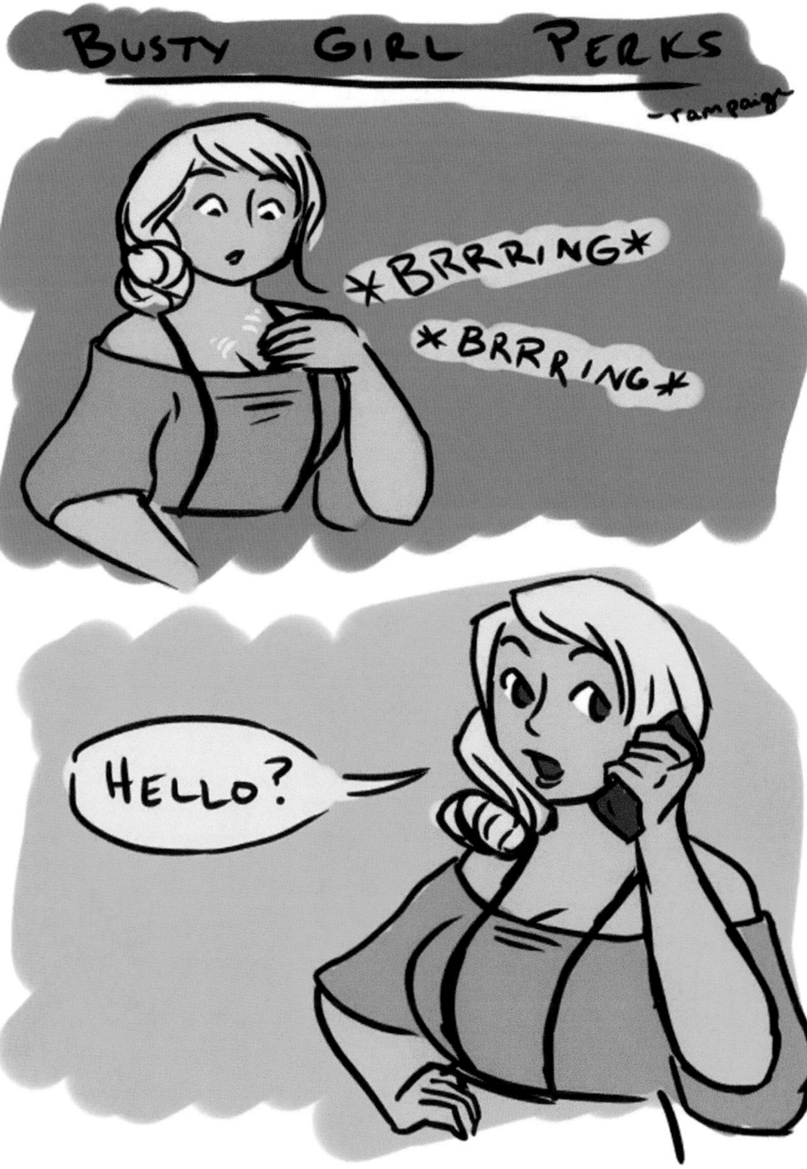
BUSTY GIRL PERKS
BRRRING
BRRRING
HELLO?

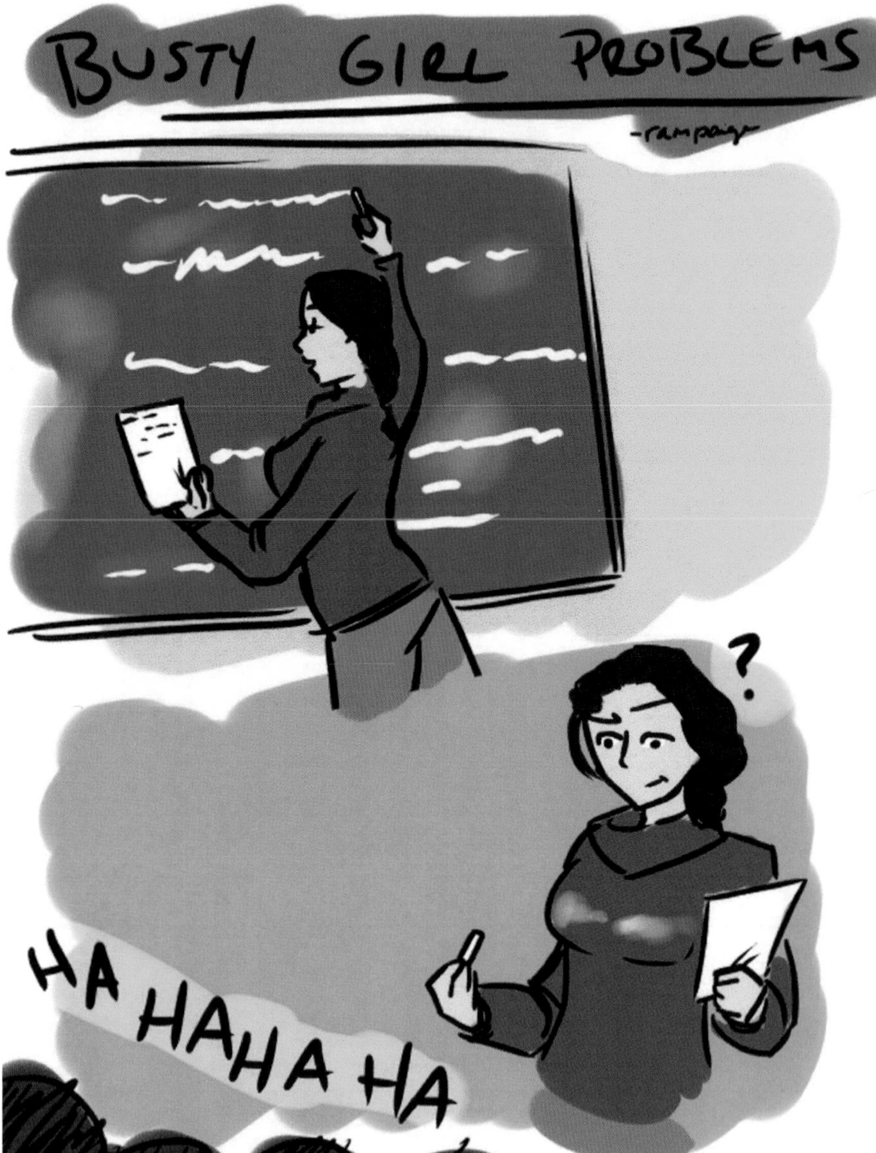
BUSTY GIRL PROBLEMS
-rampage
?
HA HAHAHA HA

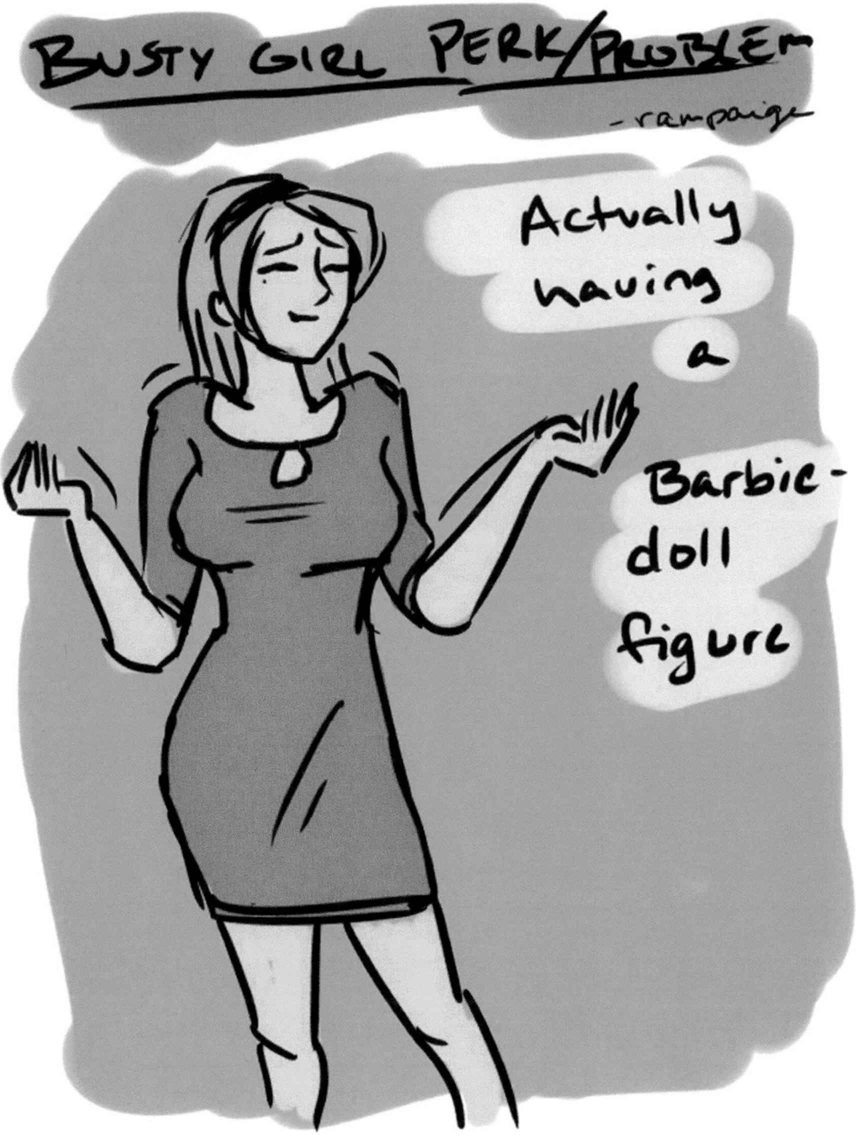
BUSTY GIRL PERK/PROBLEM
-rampaige
Actually having a Barbie-doll figure

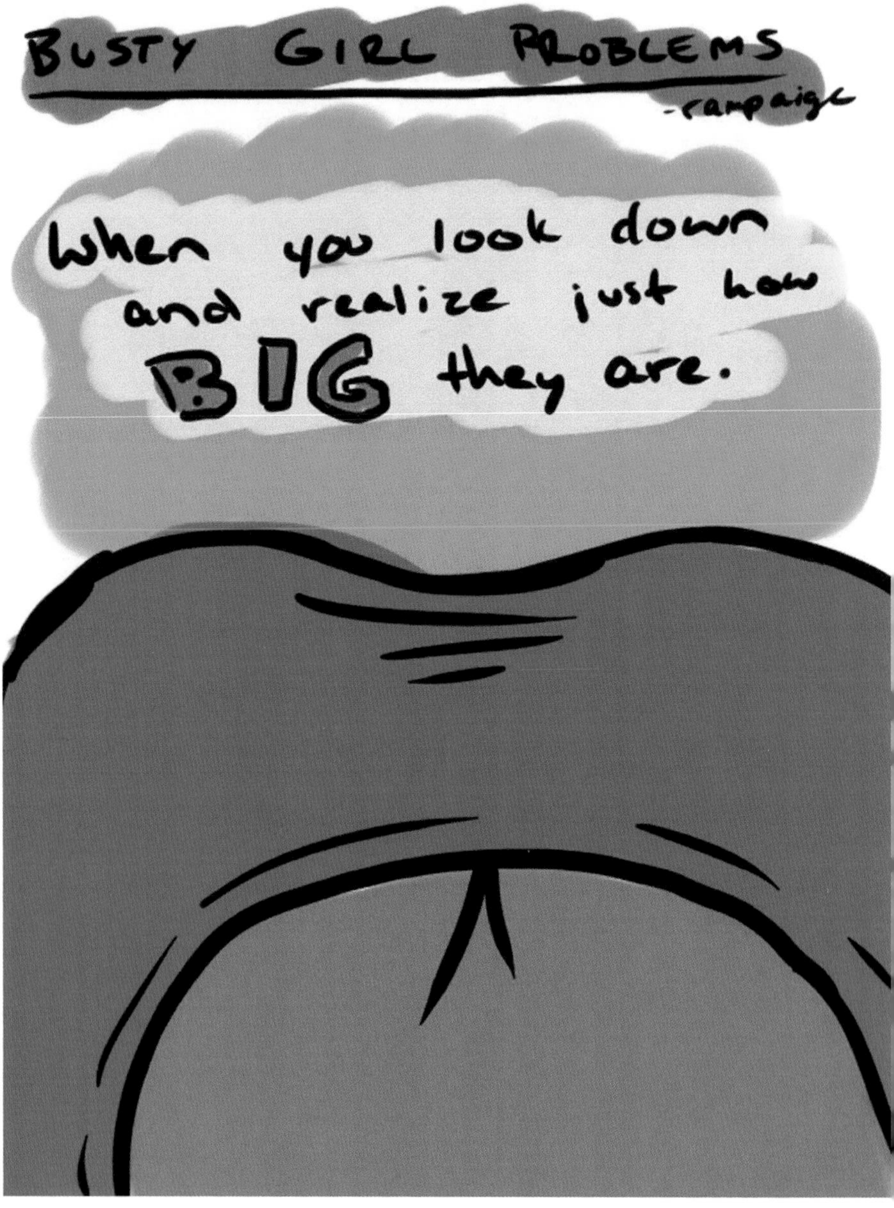
BUSTY GIRL PROBLEMS
-rampaige
When you look down and realize just how BIG they are.

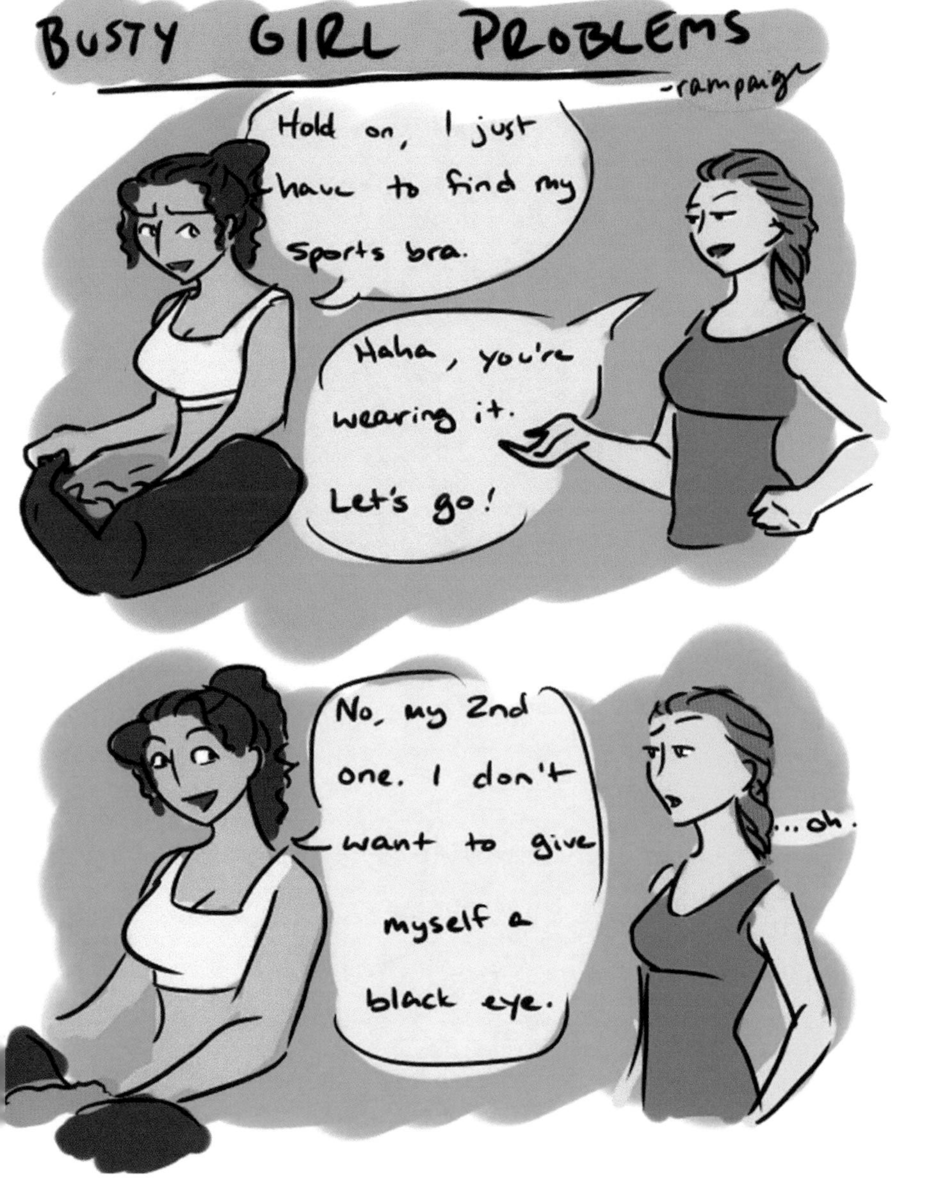

BUSTY GIRL PROBLEMS
-rampaige
Hold on, I just have to find my sports bra.
Haha, you're wearing it. Let's go!
No, my 2nd one. I don't want to give myself a black eye.
...oh.

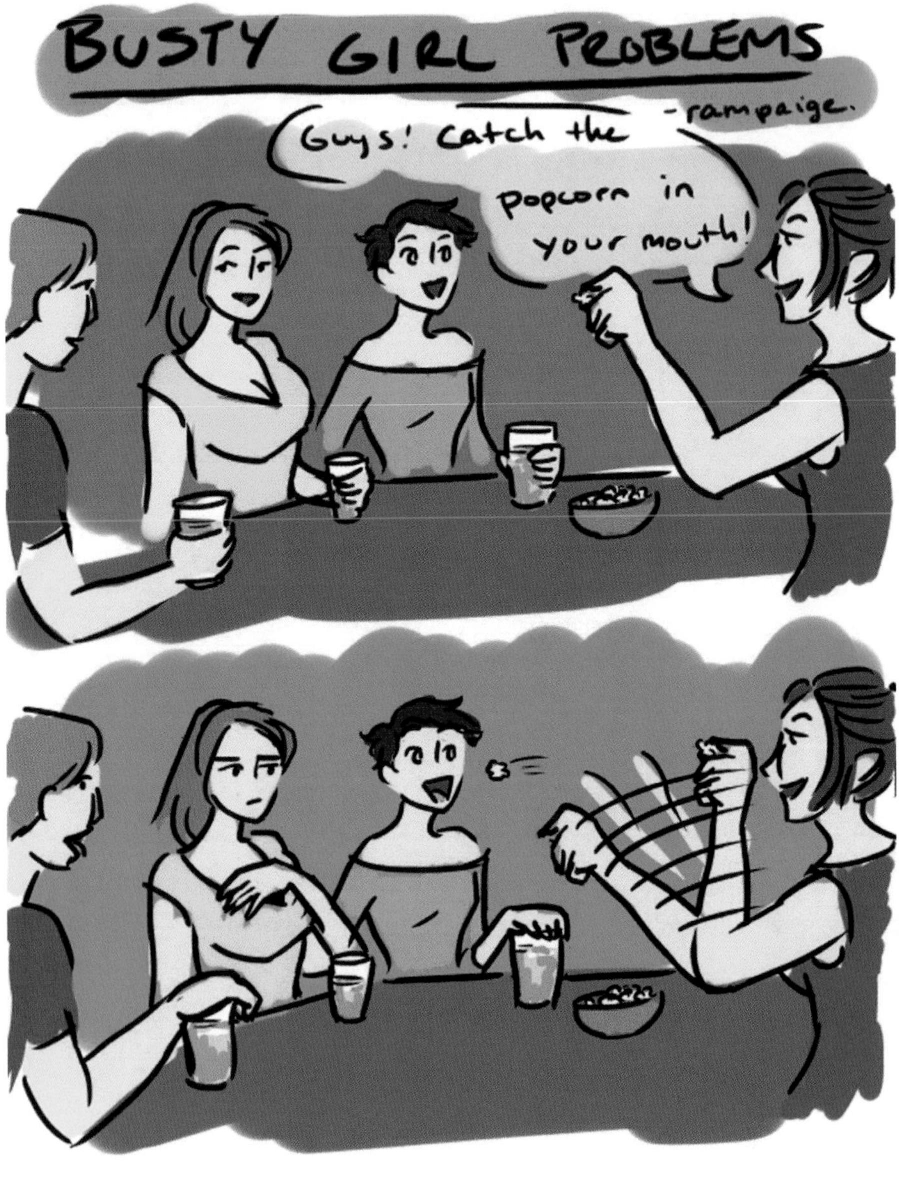
BUSTY GIRL PROBLEMS
-rampaige.
Guys! Catch the popcorn in your mouth!

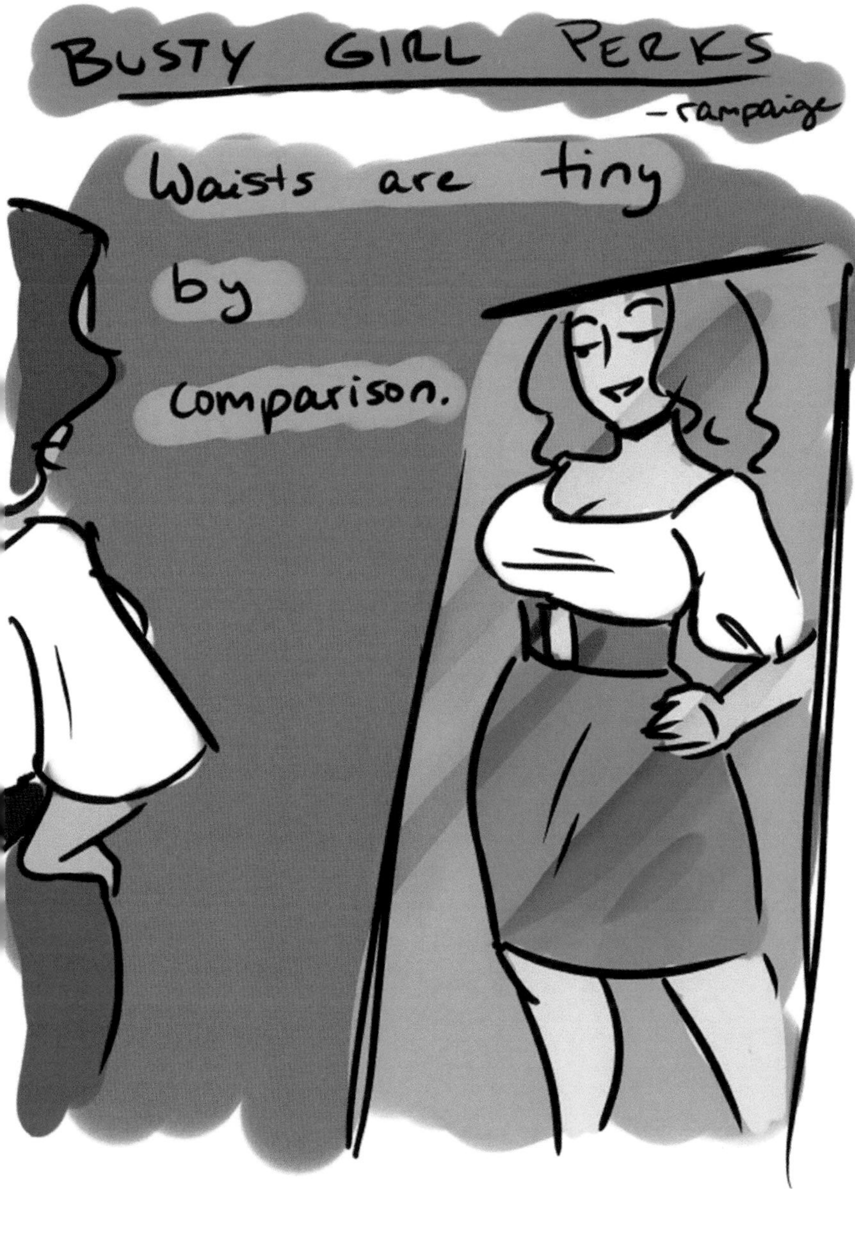
BUSTY GIRL PERKS
-rampaige
Waists are tiny
by
comparison.

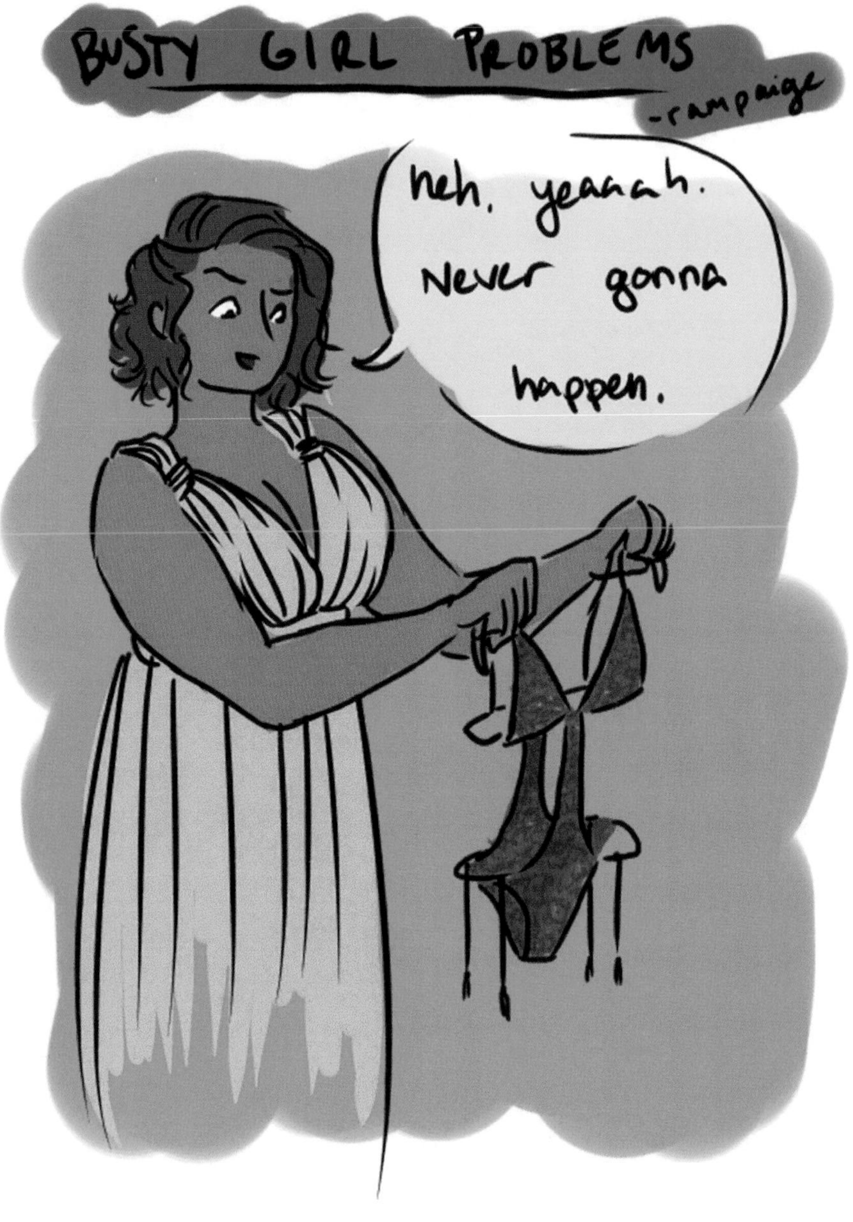
BUSTY GIRL PROBLEMS
-rampaige
neh, yeaaah.
Never gonna
happen.

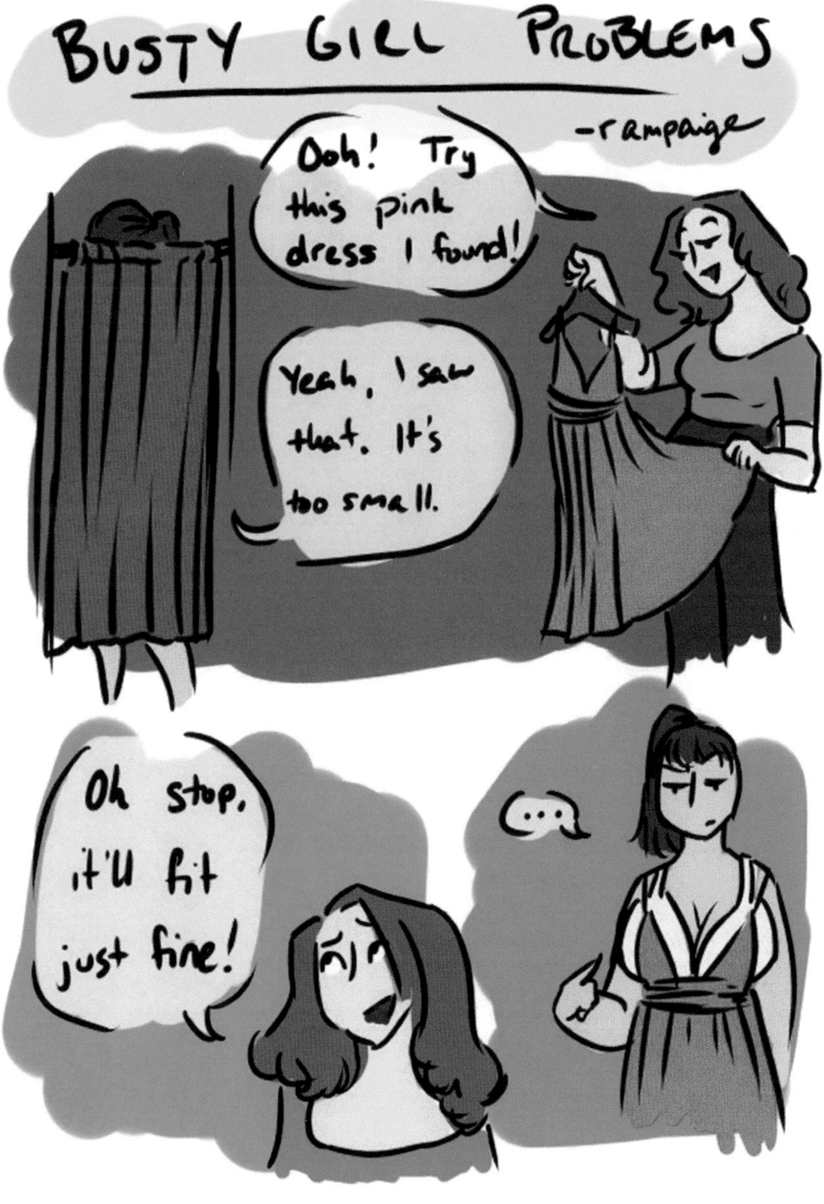
BUSTY GIRL PROBLEMS
-rampaige
Ooh! Try this pink dress I found!
Yeah, I saw that. It's too small.
Oh stop, it'll fit just fine!
...

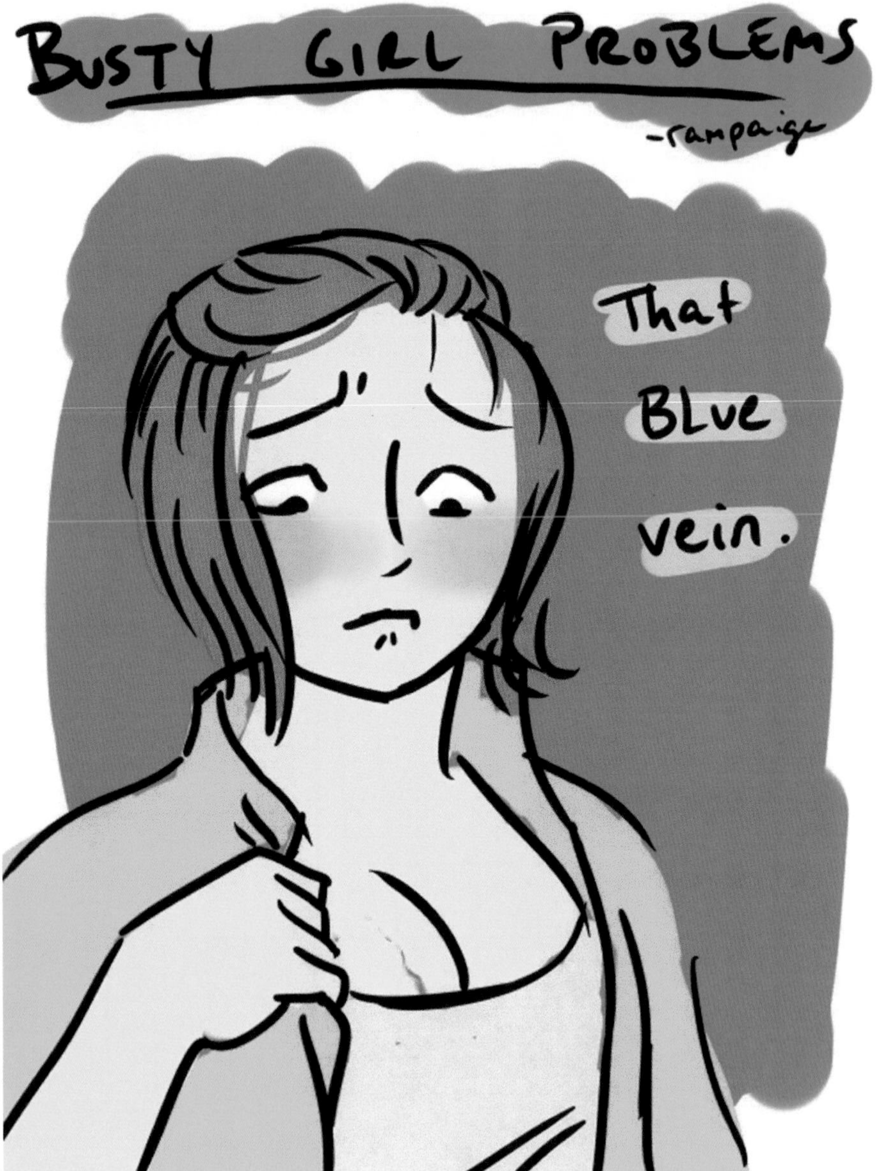
BUSTY GIRL PROBLEMS
-rampaige
That
Blue
vein.

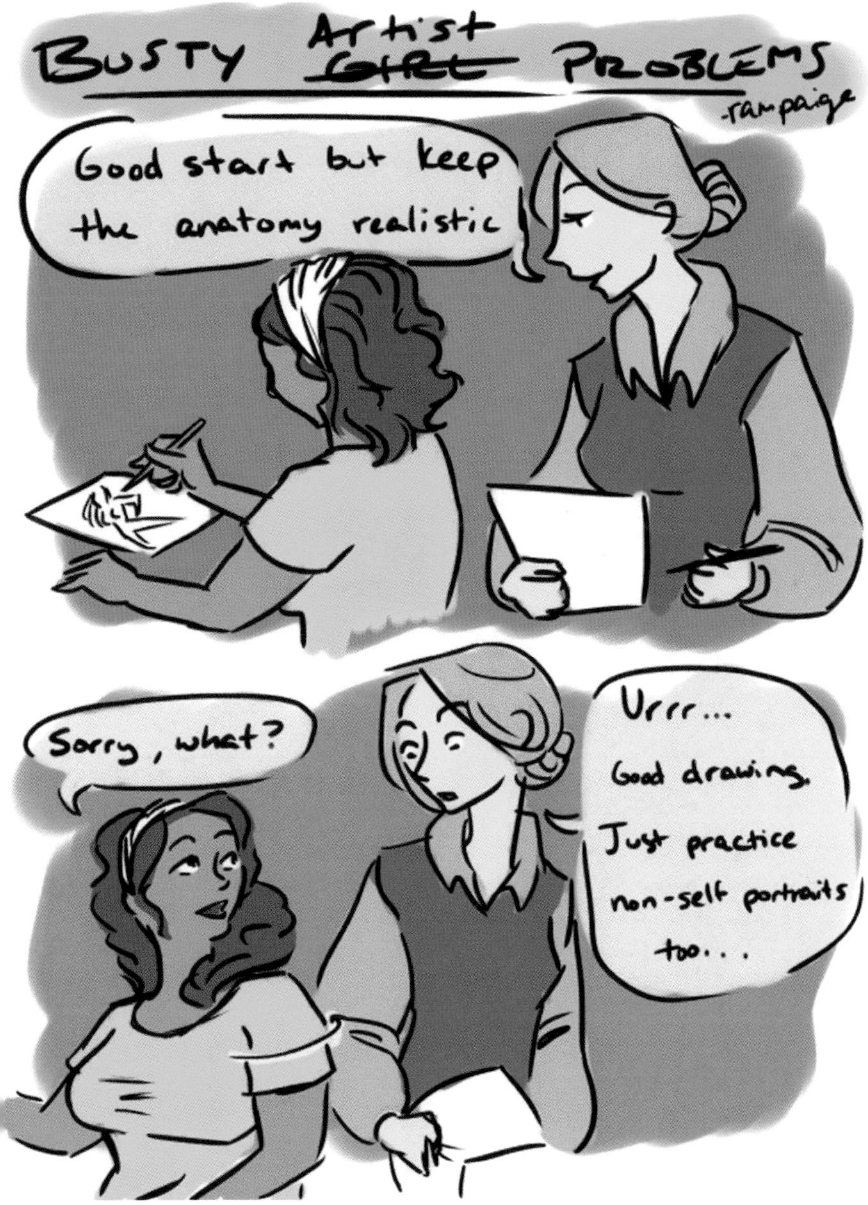
BUSTY ~~GIRL~~ Artist PROBLEMS
-rampaige
Good start but keep the anatomy realistic
Sorry, what?
Urrr... Good drawing. Just practice non-self portraits too...

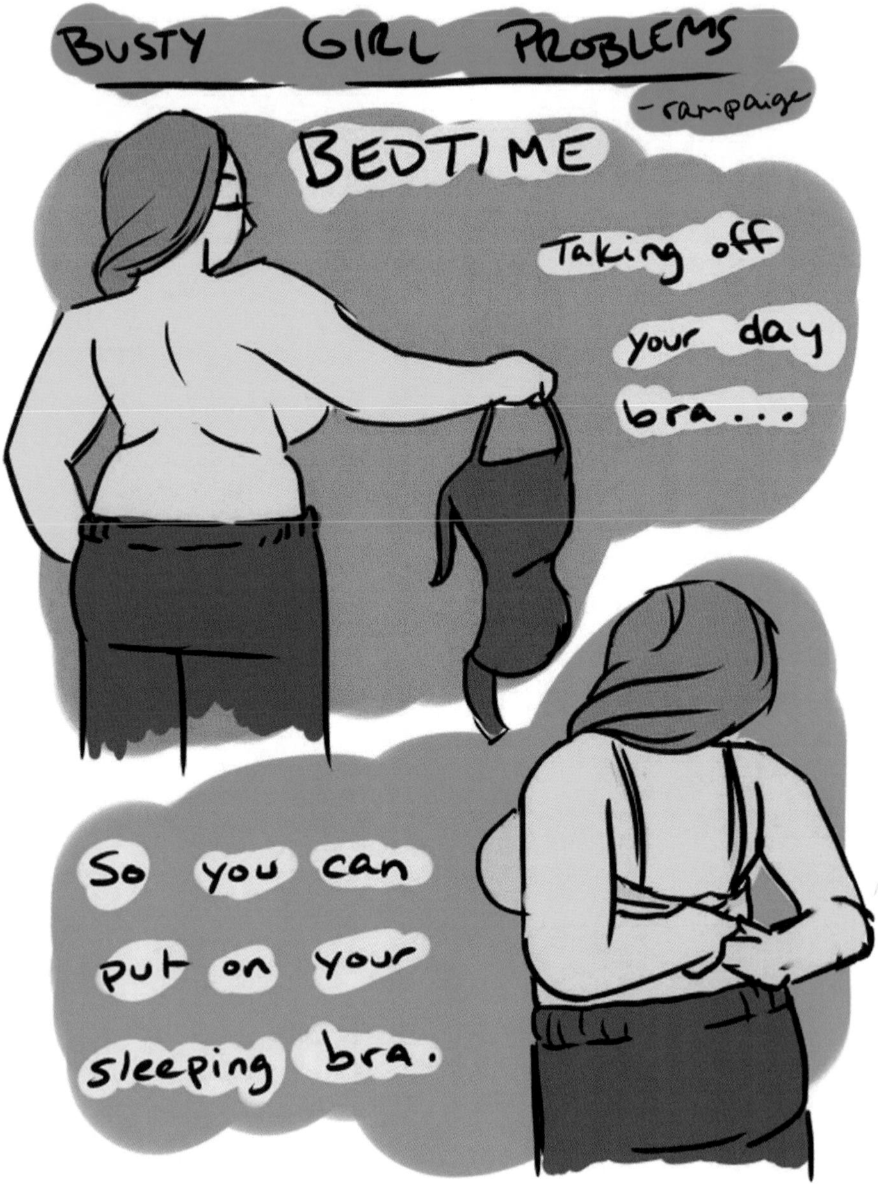
BUSTY GIRL PROBLEMS
-rampaige
BEDTIME
Taking off your day bra....
So you can put on your sleeping bra.

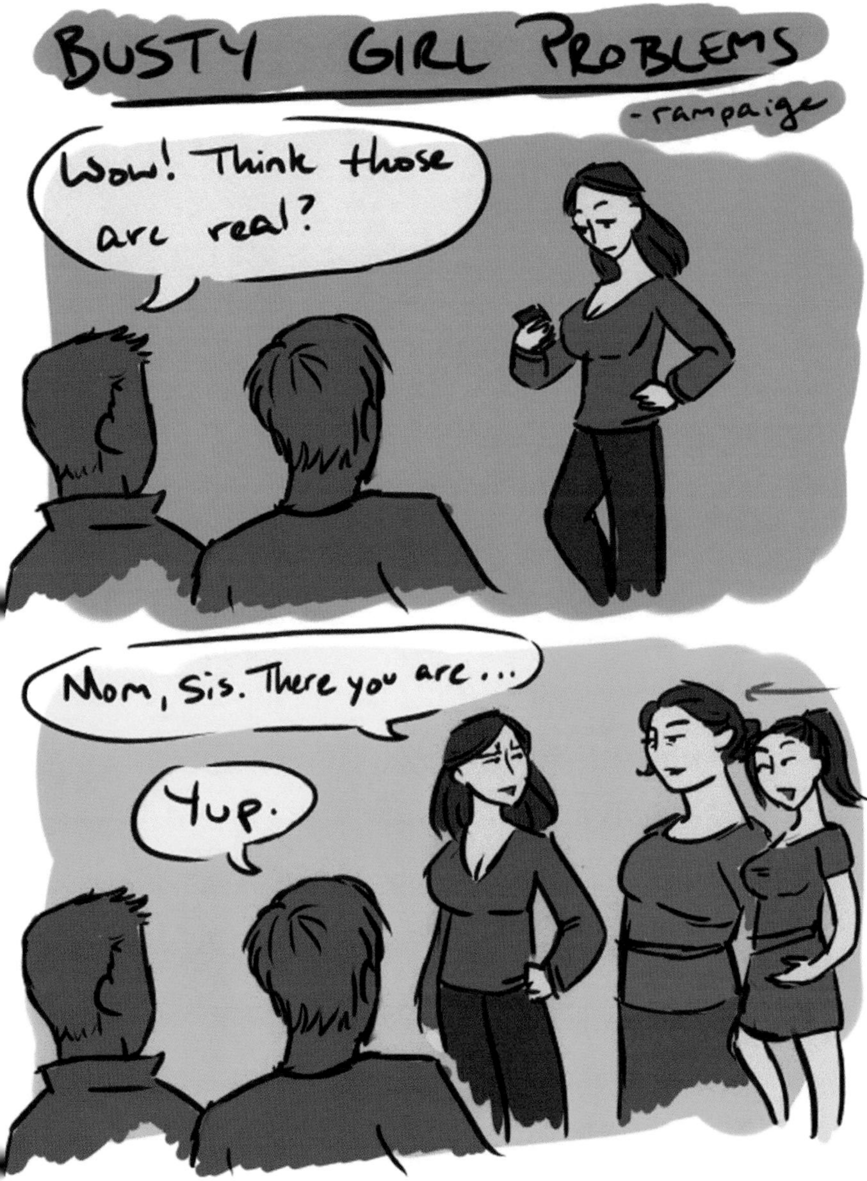
BUSTY GIRL PROBLEMS
-rampaige
Wow! Think those are real?
Mom, Sis. There you are...
Yup.

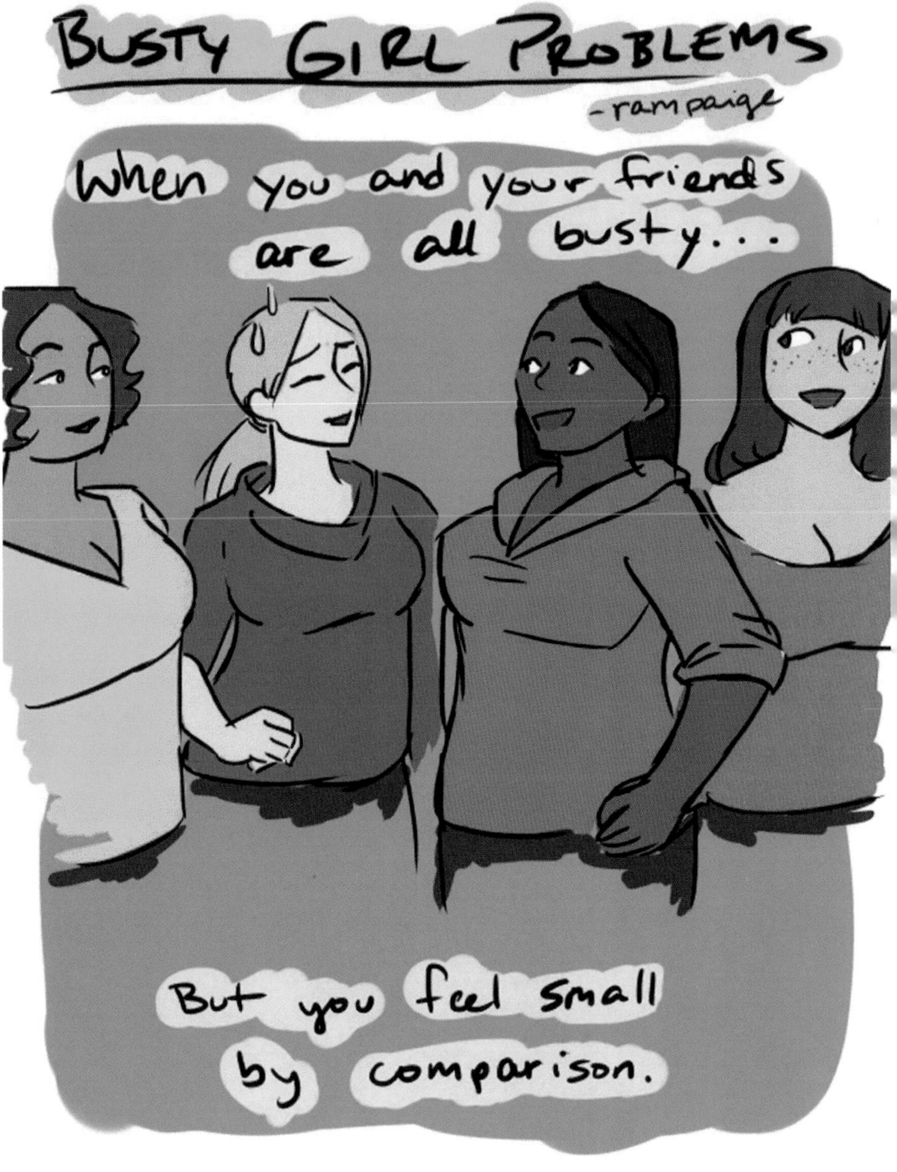
BUSTY GIRL PROBLEMS
-rampaige
When you and your friends are all busty...
But you feel small by comparison.

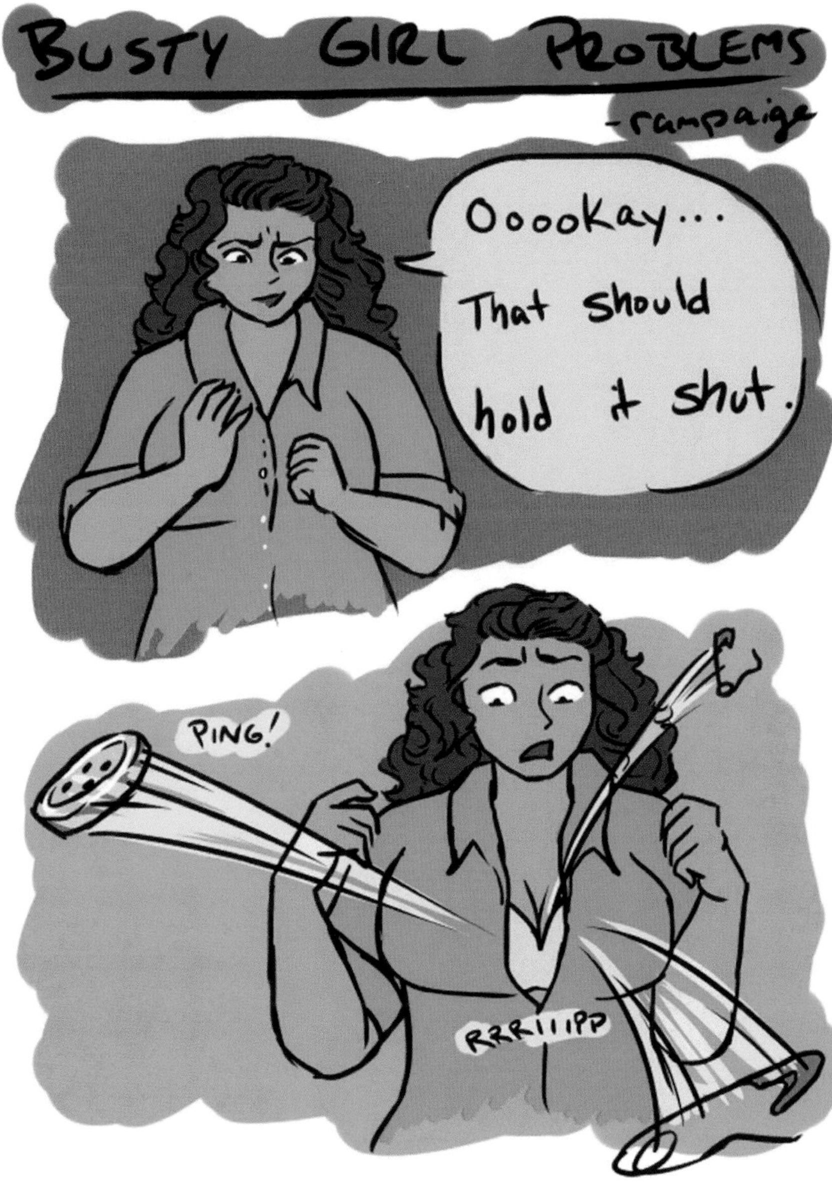
BUSTY GIRL PROBLEMS
-rampaige
Ooookay...
That should hold it shut.
PING!
RRRIIIPP

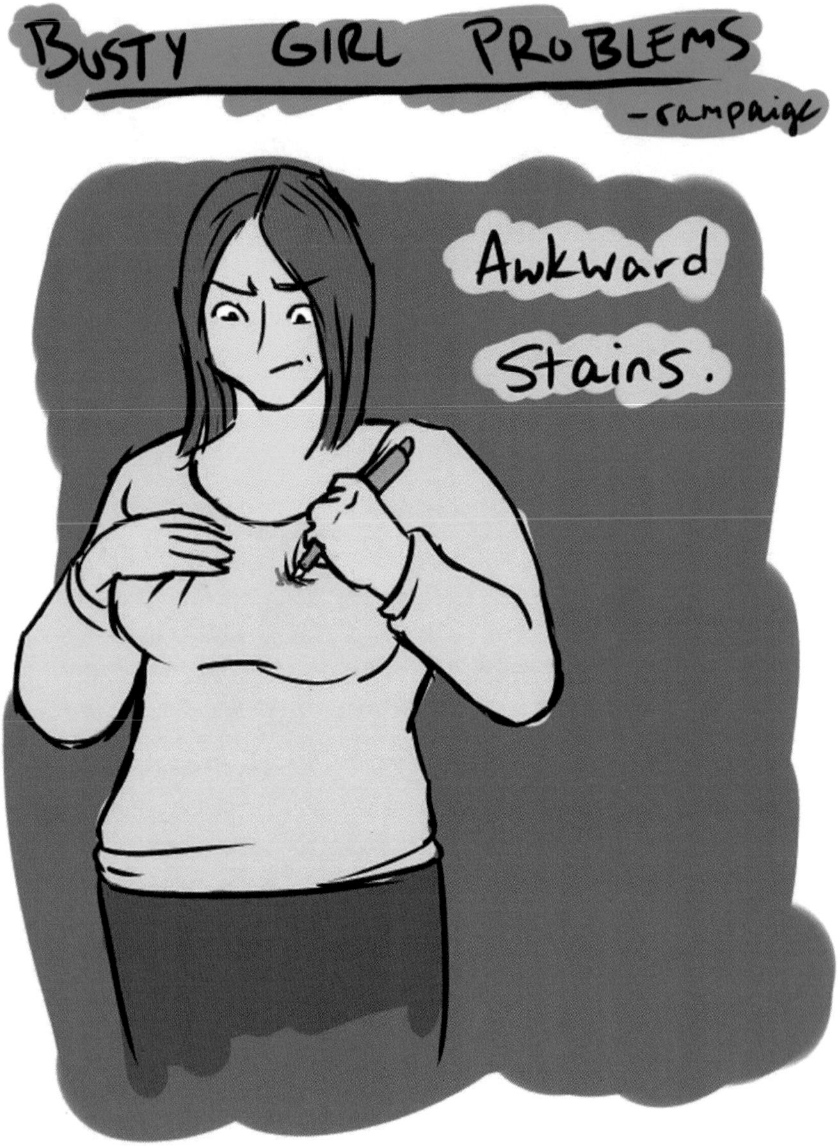
BUSTY GIRL PROBLEMS
-rampaige
Awkward Stains.

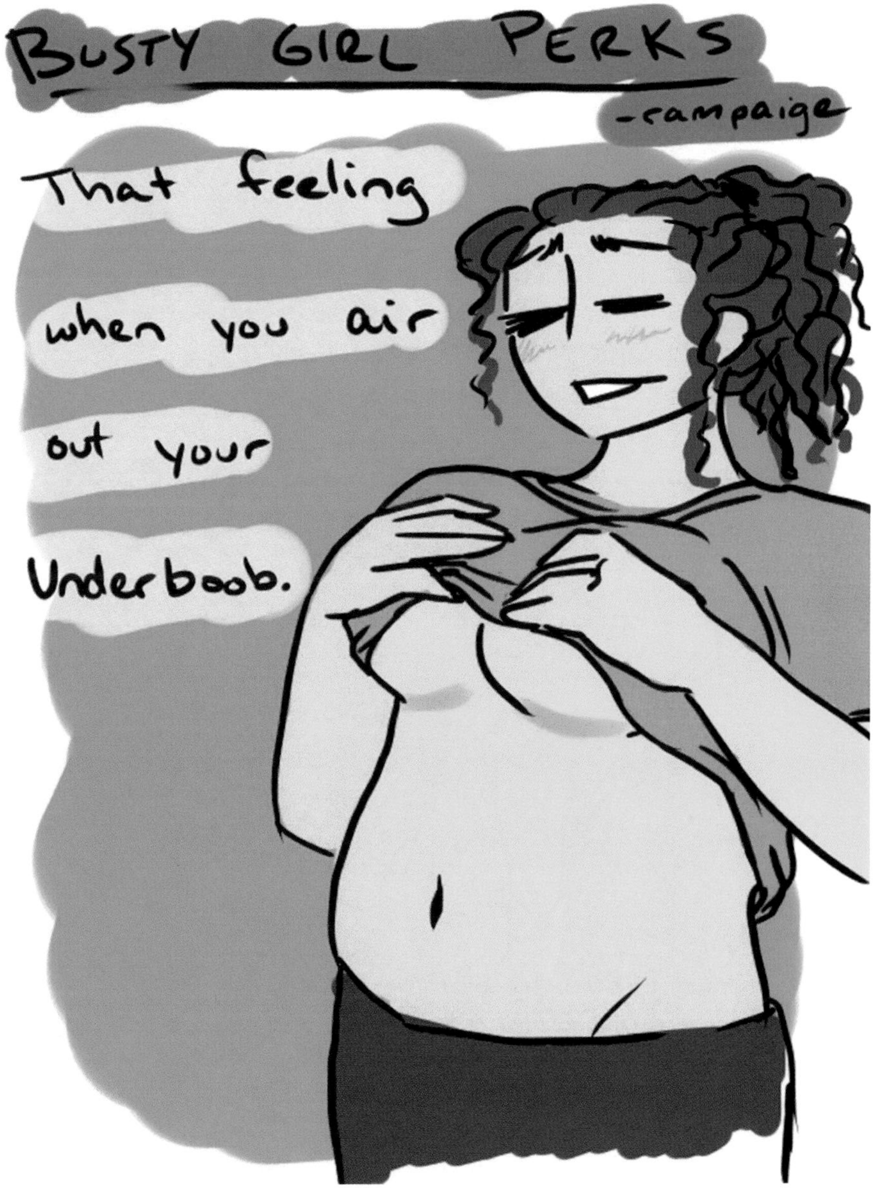
BUSTY GIRL PERKS
-campaige
That feeling
when you air
out your
Underboob.

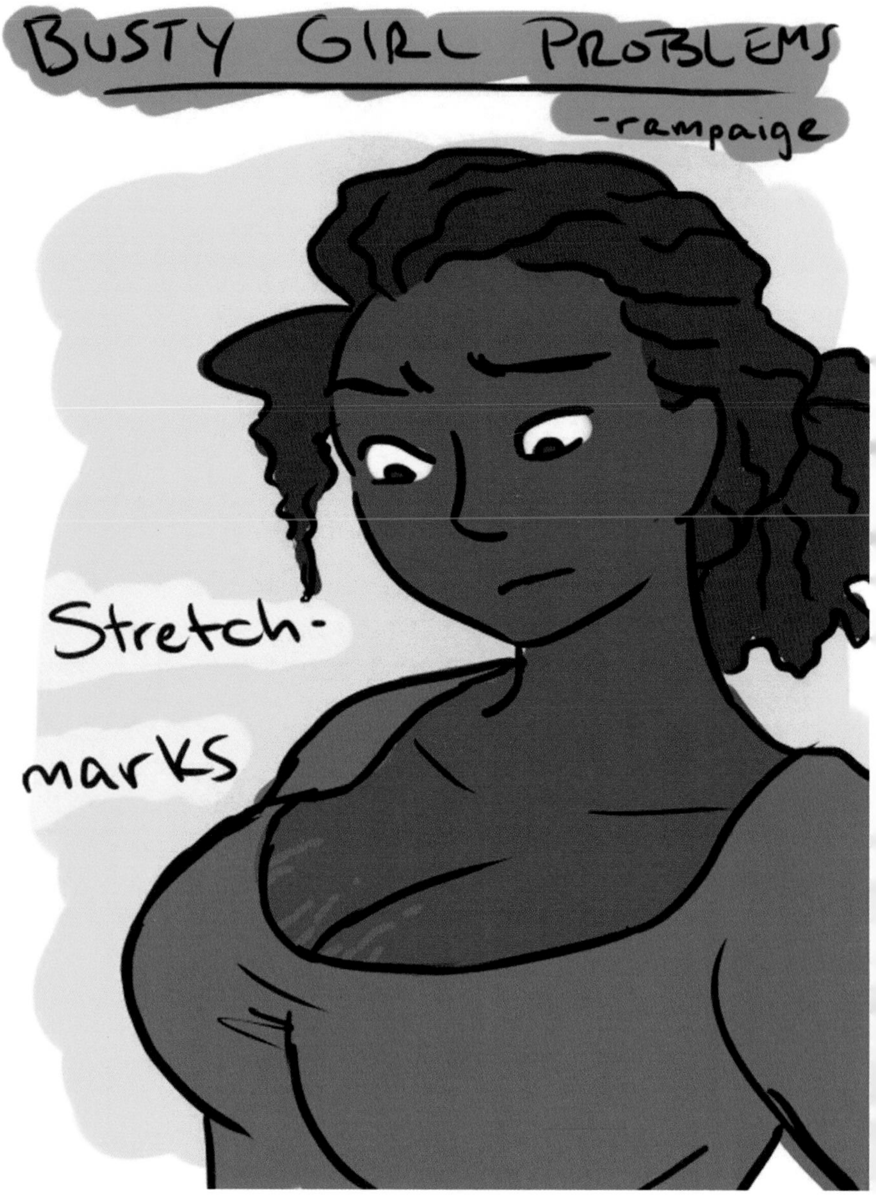
BUSTY GIRL PROBLEMS
-rampaige
Stretch-
marks

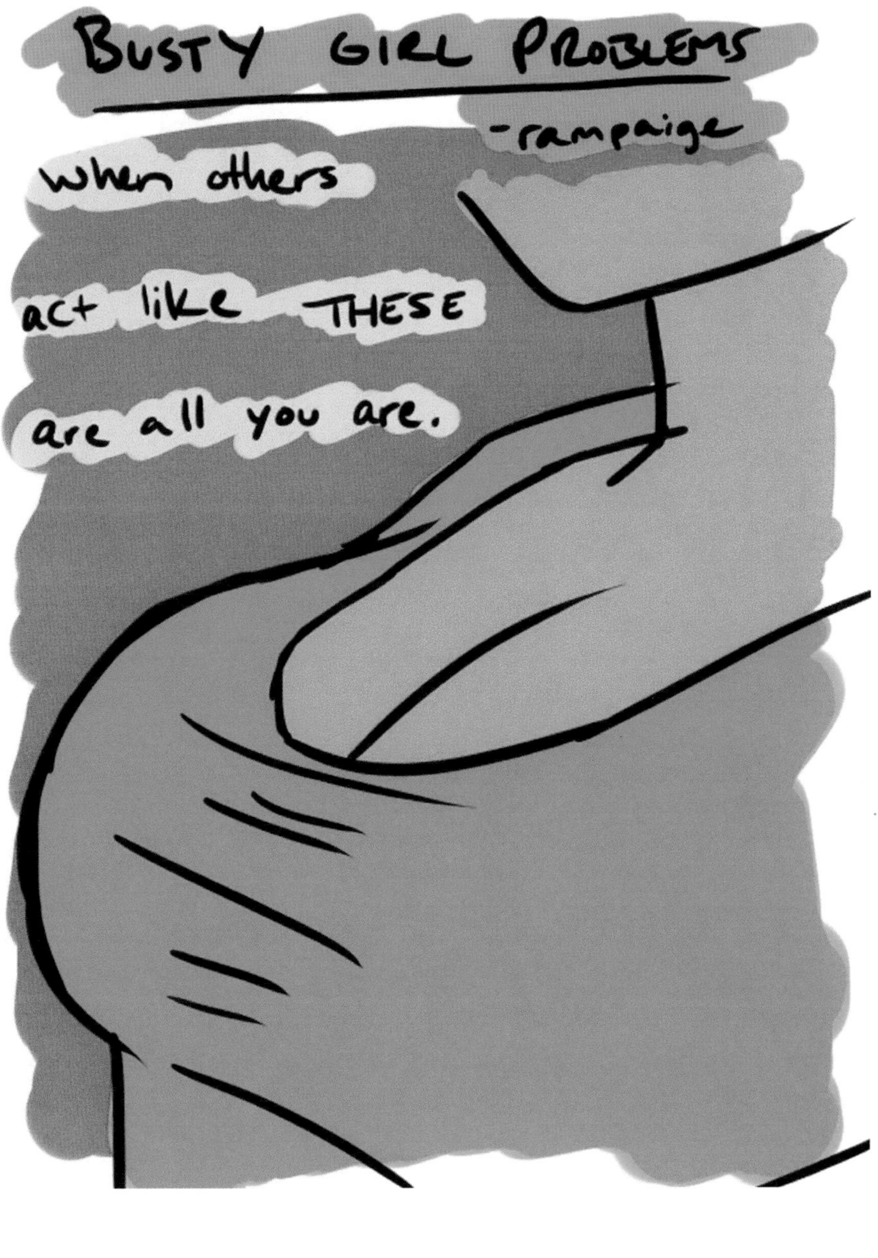
BUSTY GIRL PROBLEMS
-rampaige
when others
act like THESE
are all you are.

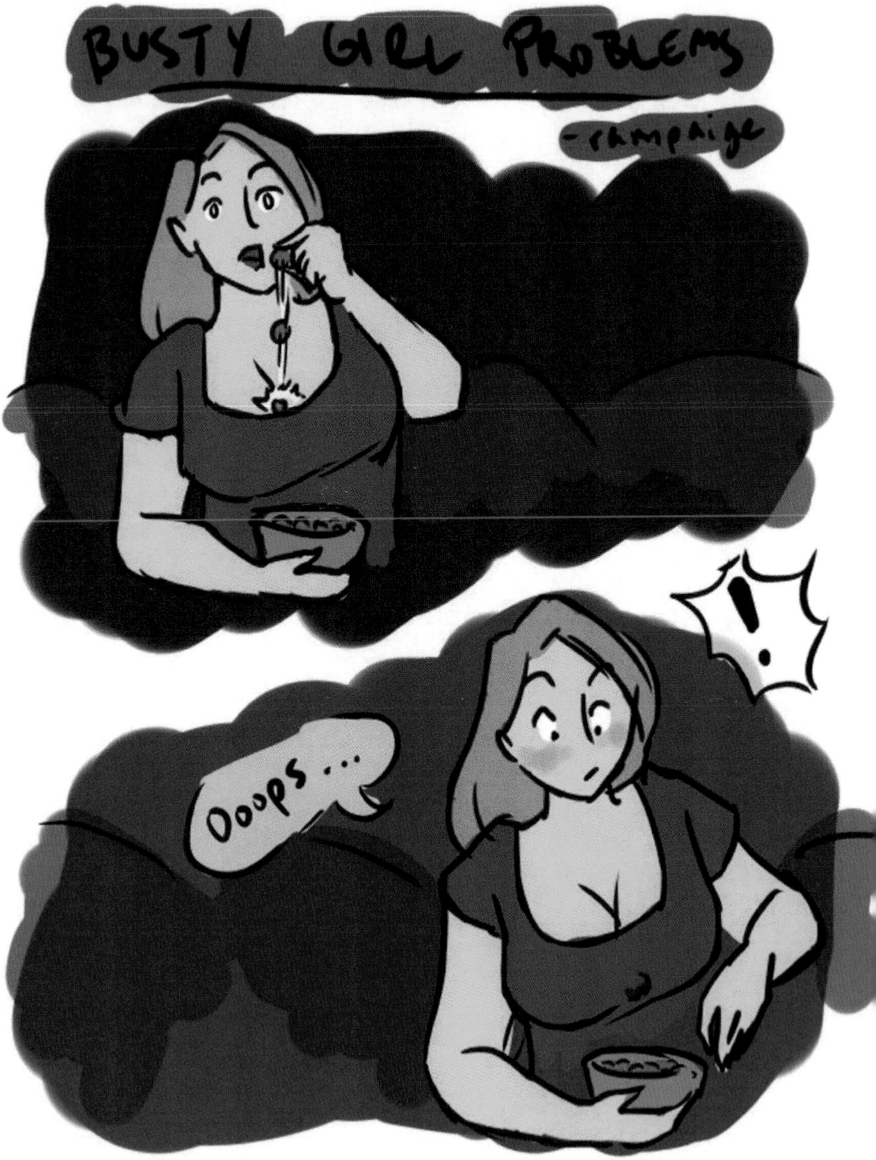
BUSTY GIRL PROBLEMS
-rampaige
!
Ooops...

BUSTY GIRL PROBLEMS

-rampaige

CLICK

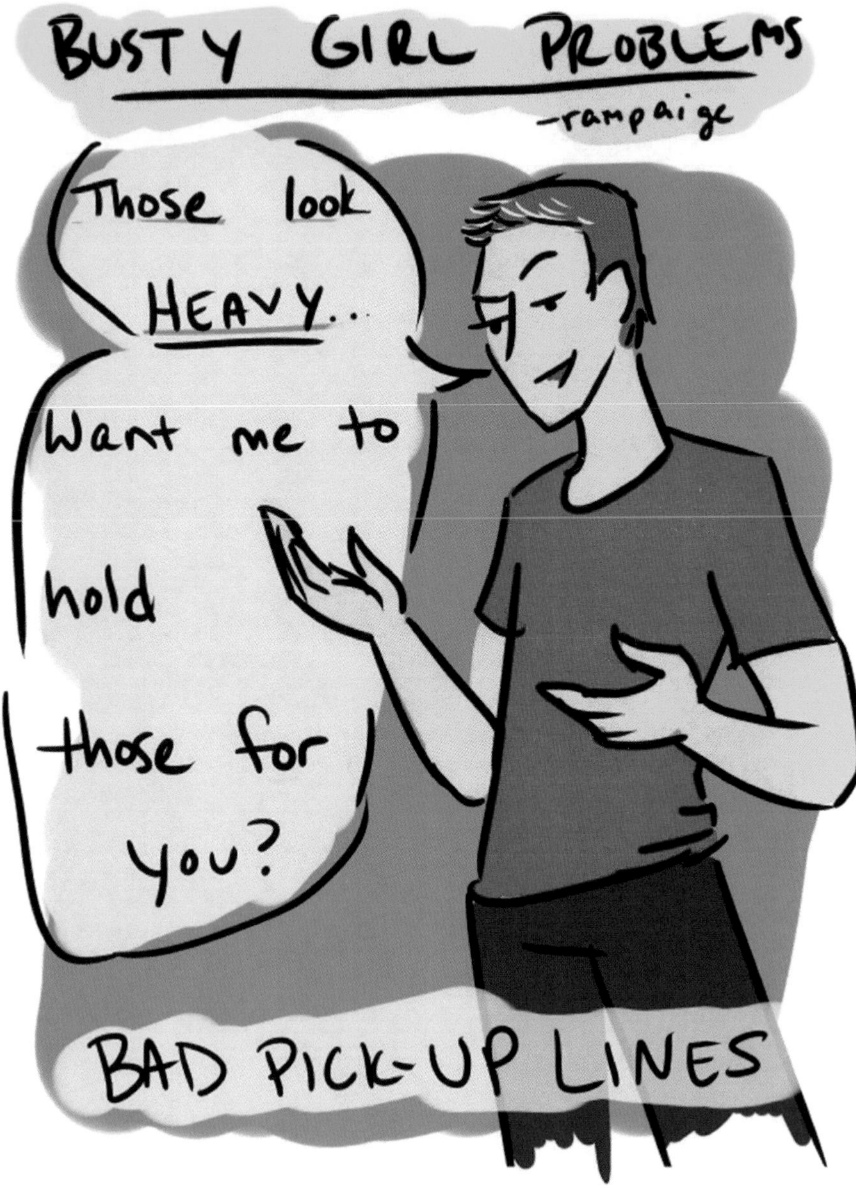
BUSTY GIRL PROBLEMS
-rampaige
Those look HEAVY...
Want me to hold those for you?
BAD PICK-UP LINES

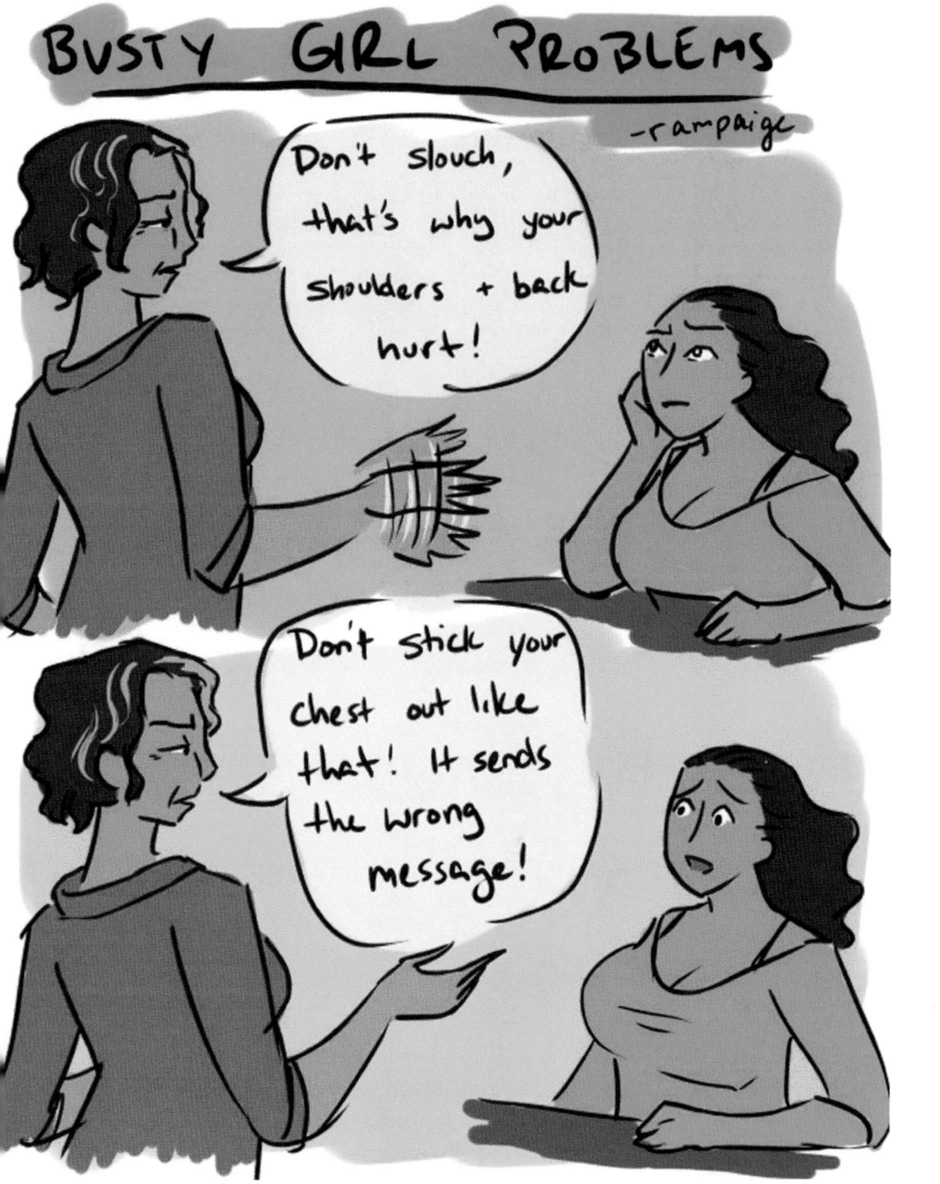
BUSTY GIRL PROBLEMS
-rampaige
Don't slouch, that's why your shoulders + back hurt!
Don't stick your chest out like that! It sends the wrong message!

BUSTY GIRL PROBLEMS

-rampaige

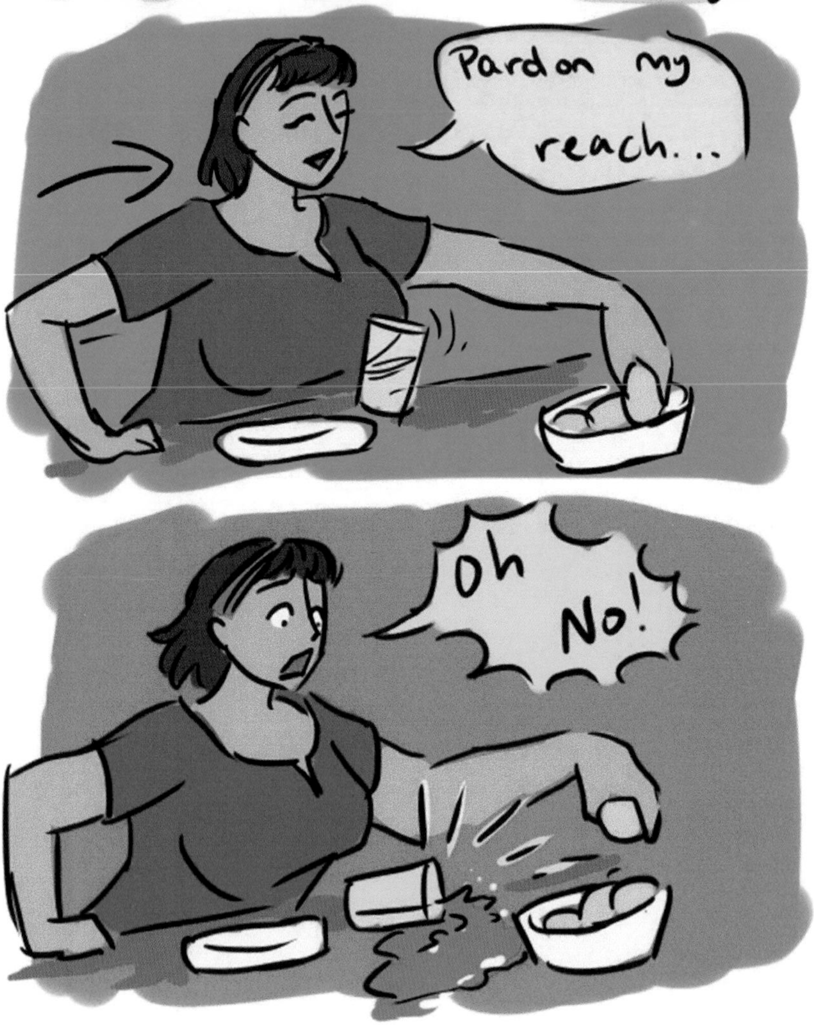

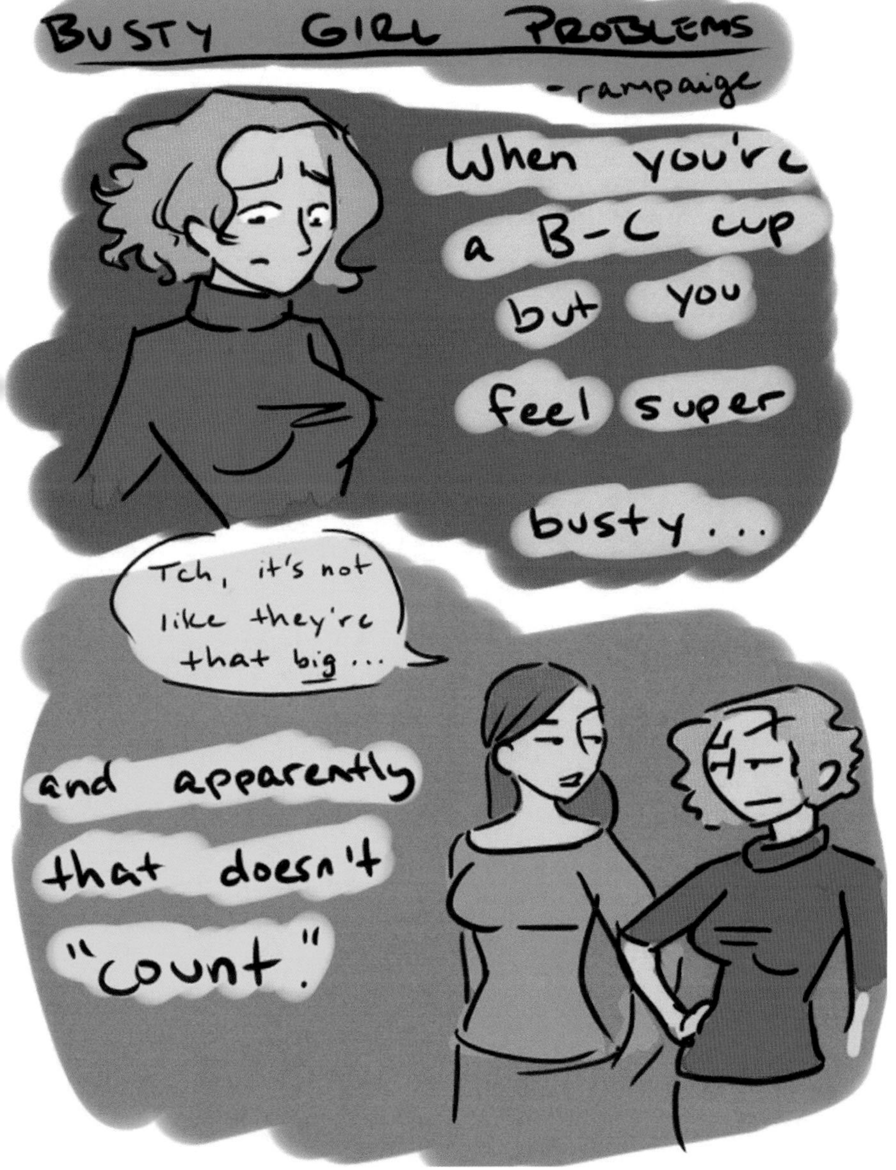
BUSTY GIRL PROBLEMS
-rampaige
When you're a B-C cup but you feel super busty...
Tch, it's not like they're that big...
and apparently that doesn't "count."

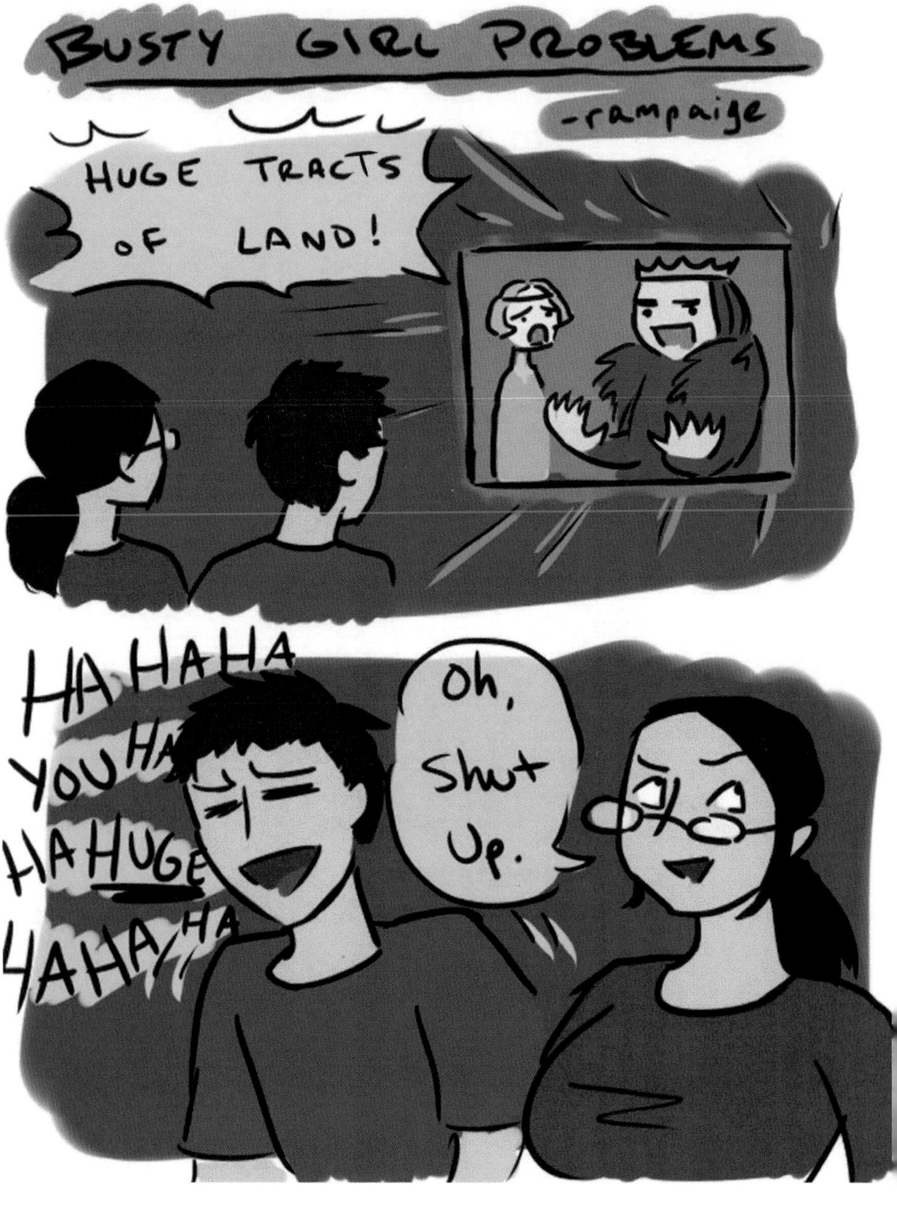

BUSTY GIRL PROBLEMS
-rampaige
HUGE TRACTS OF LAND!
HA HAHA YOU HA HA HUGE HAHAHA HA
Oh, Shut Up.

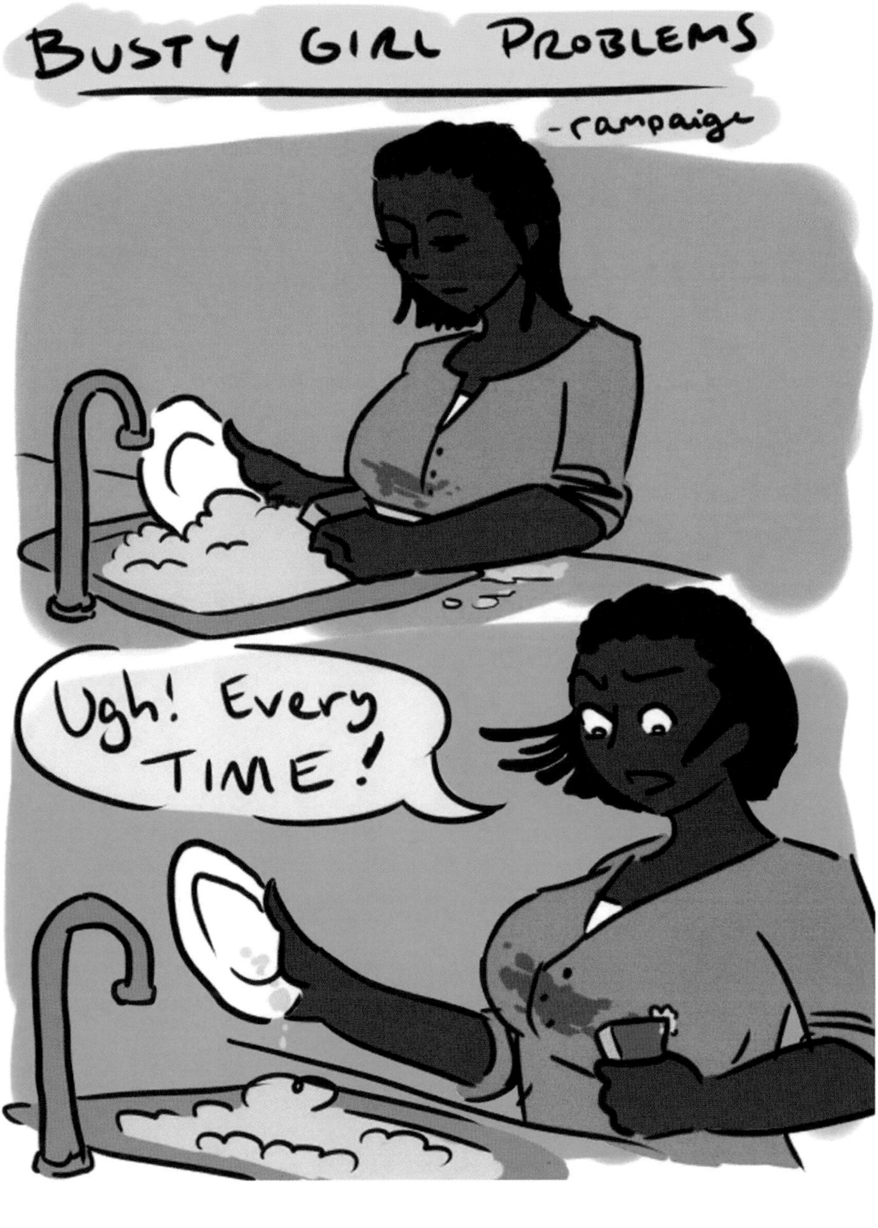
BUSTY GIRL PROBLEMS
-rampaige
Ugh! Every TIME!

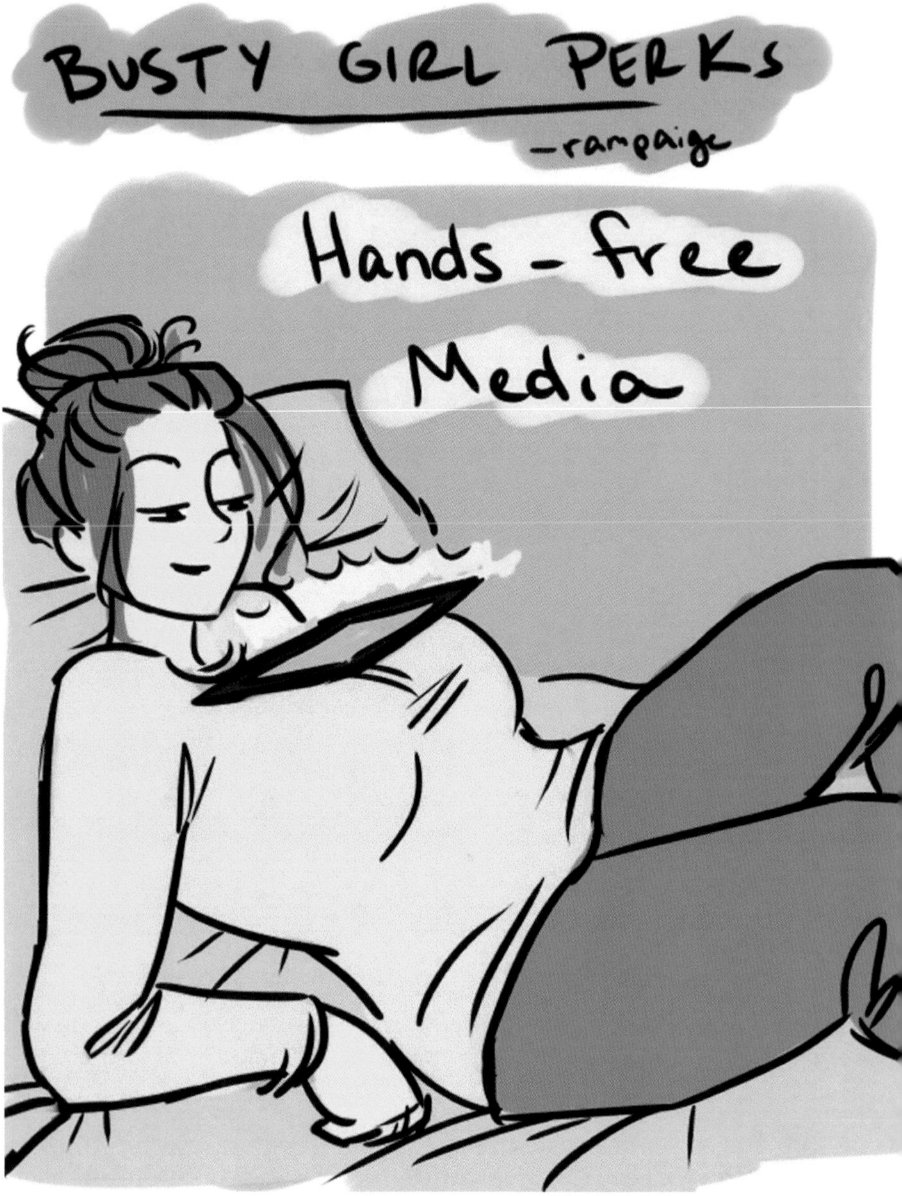
BUSTY GIRL PERKS
-rampaige
Hands-free Media

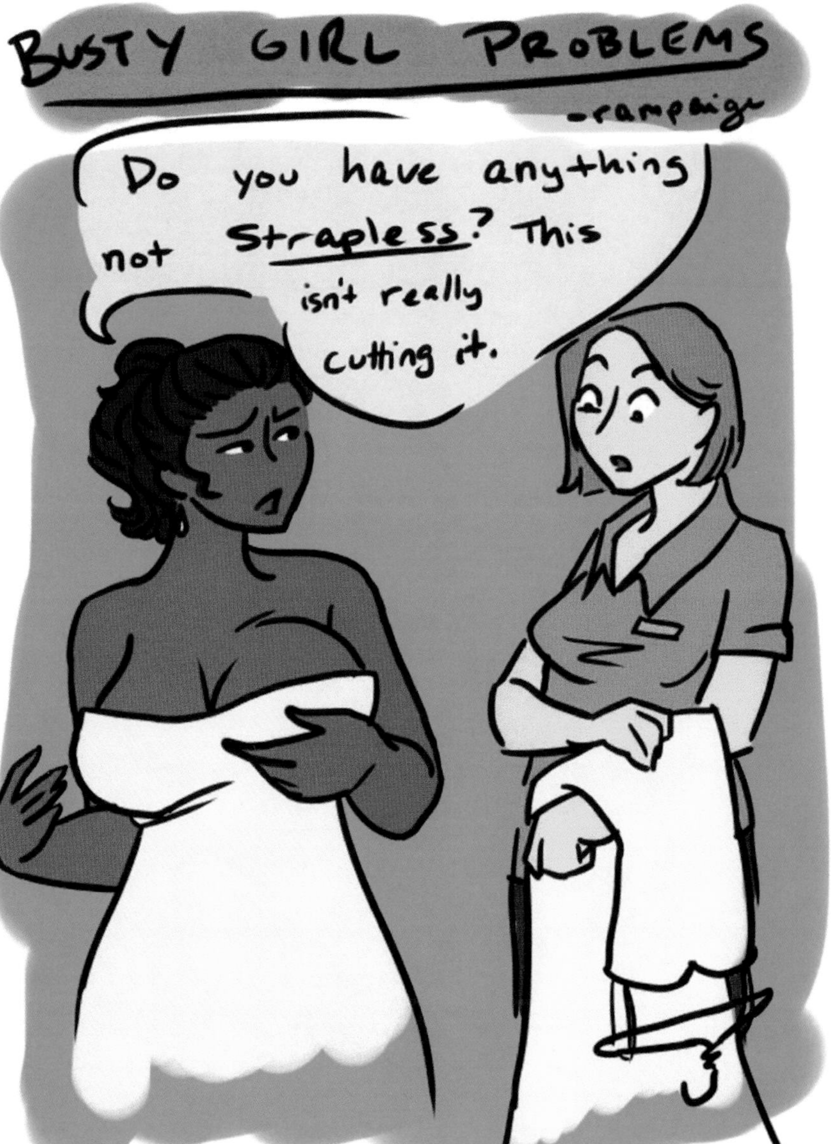
BUSTY GIRL PROBLEMS
-rampaige
Do you have anything not strapless? This isn't really cutting it.

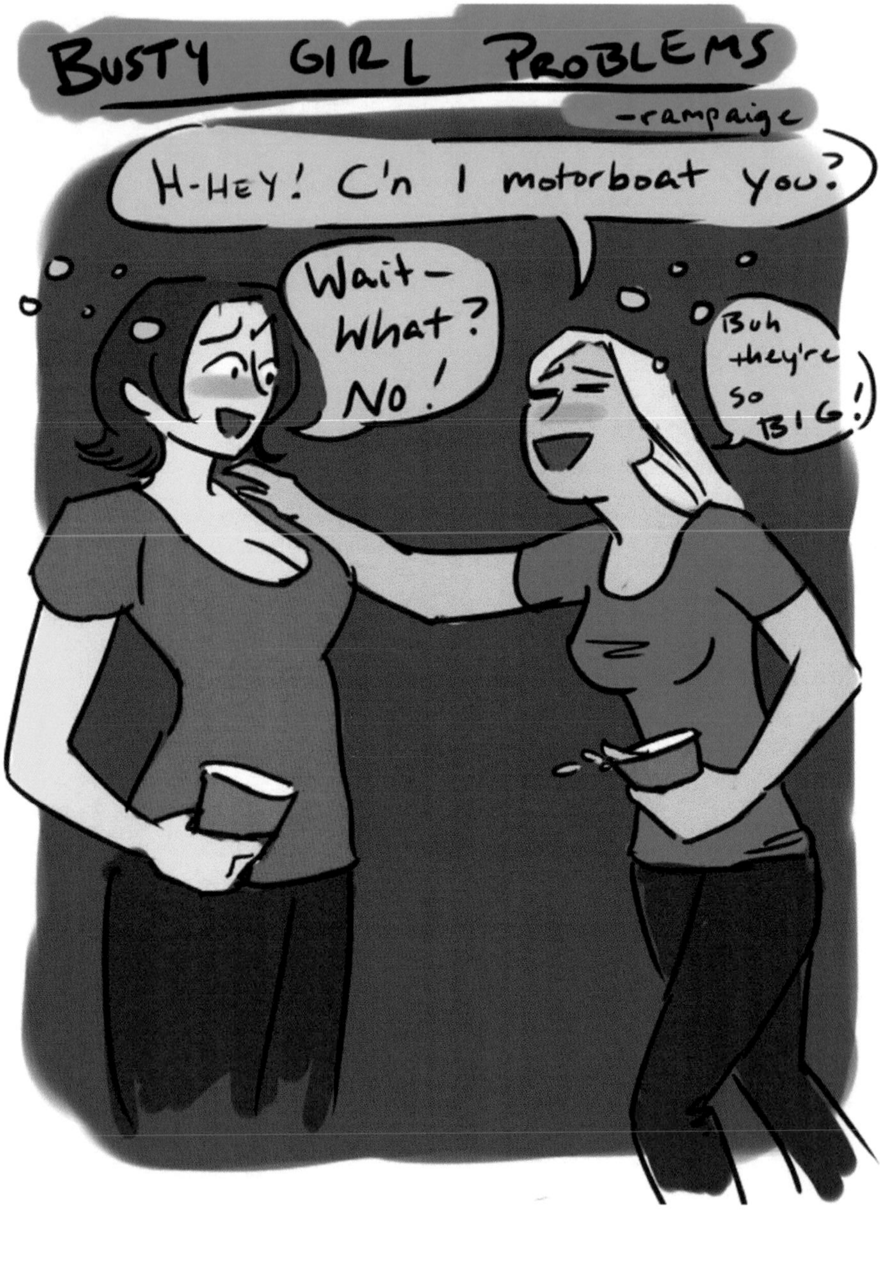
BUSTY GIRL PROBLEMS
-rampaige
H-HEY! C'n I motorboat you?
Wait- What? No!
Buh they're so BIG!

BUSTY GIRL PROBLEMS

-rampaige

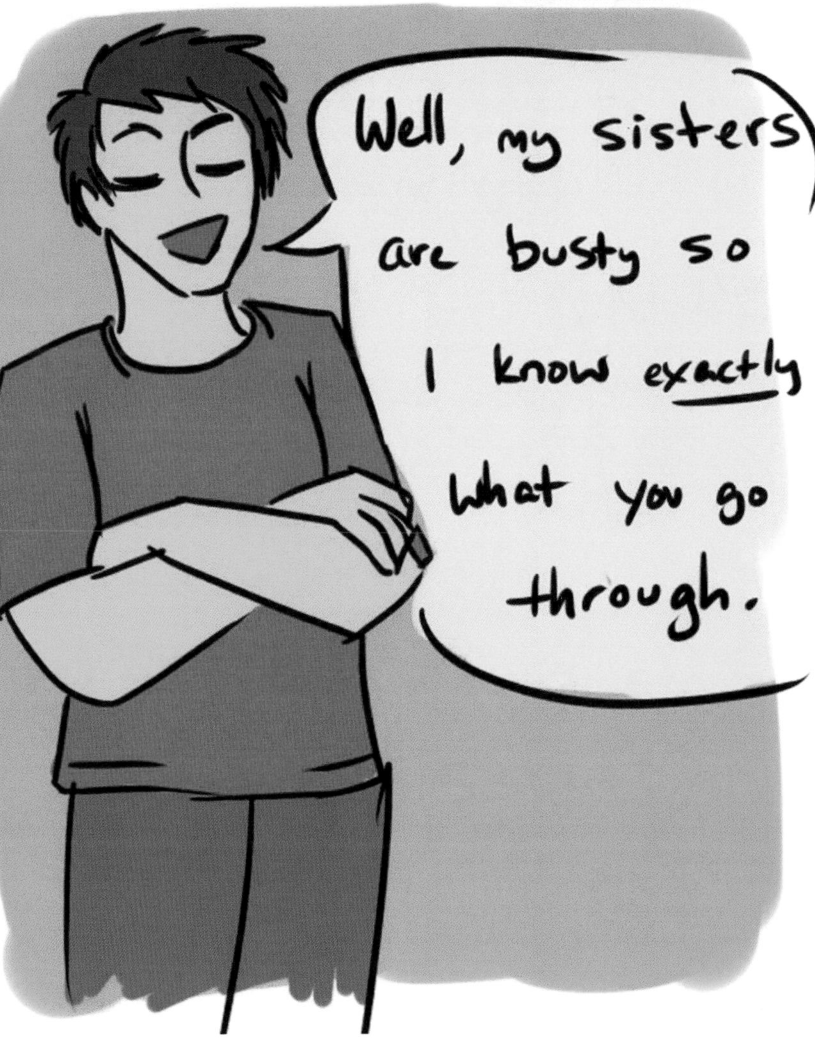

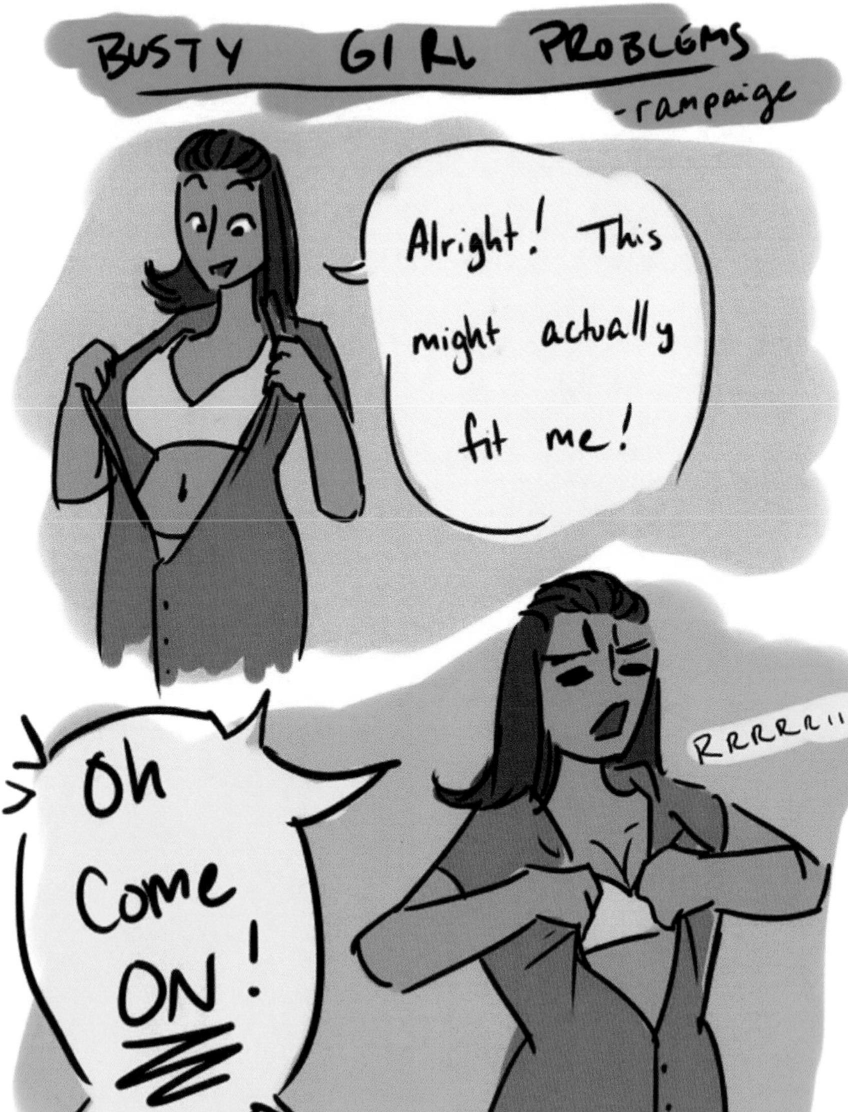
BUSTY GIRL PROBLEMS
-rampaige
Alright! This might actually fit me!
RRRRRiiip
Oh Come ON!

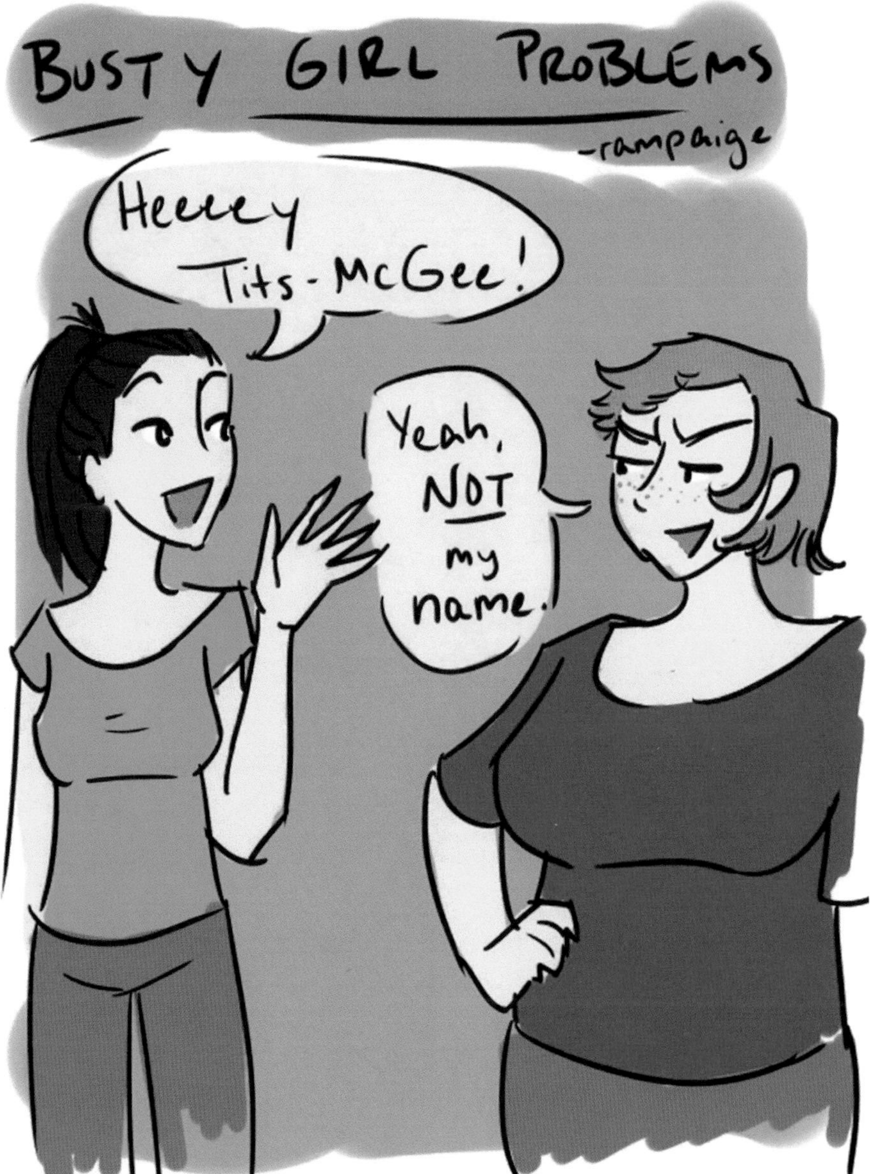
BUSTY GIRL PROBLEMS
-rampaige
Heeeey Tits-McGee!
Yeah, NOT my name.

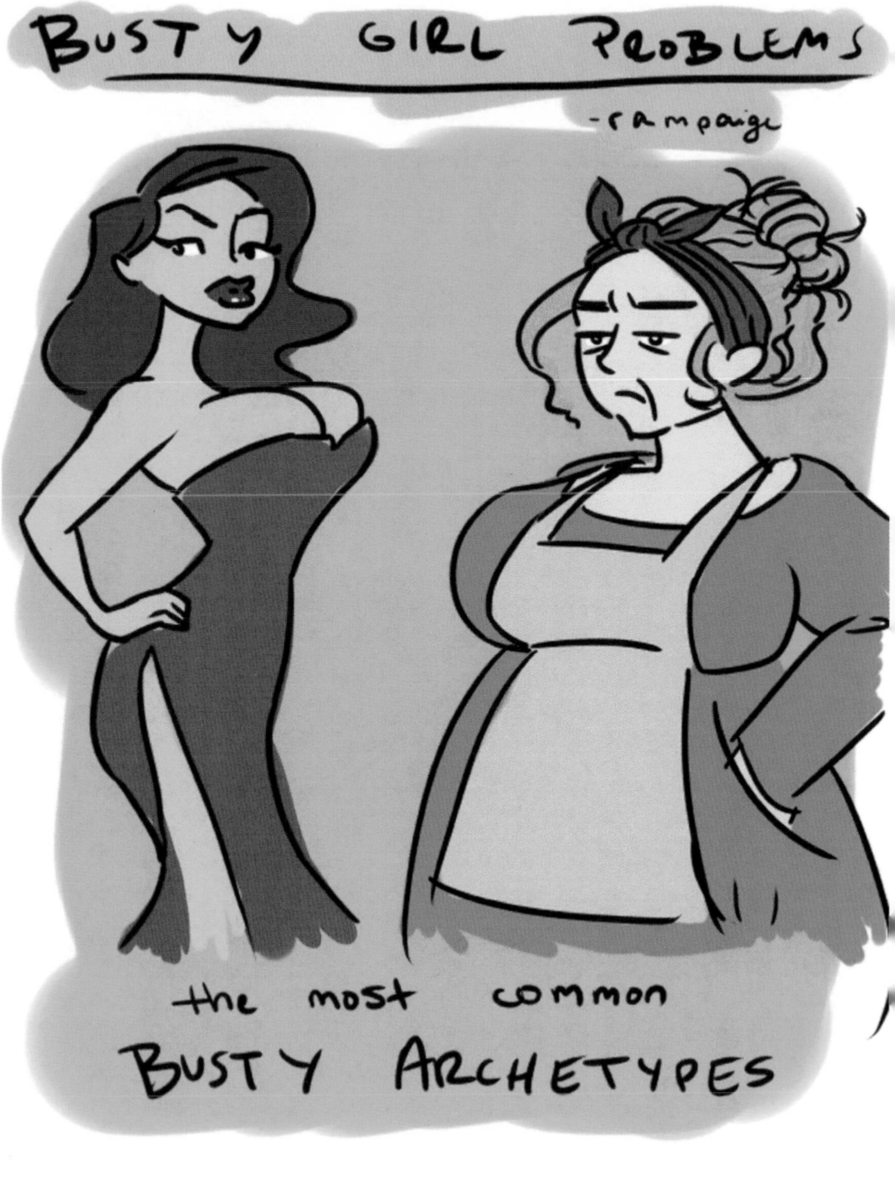
BUSTY GIRL PROBLEMS
-rampaige
the most common
BUSTY ARCHETYPES

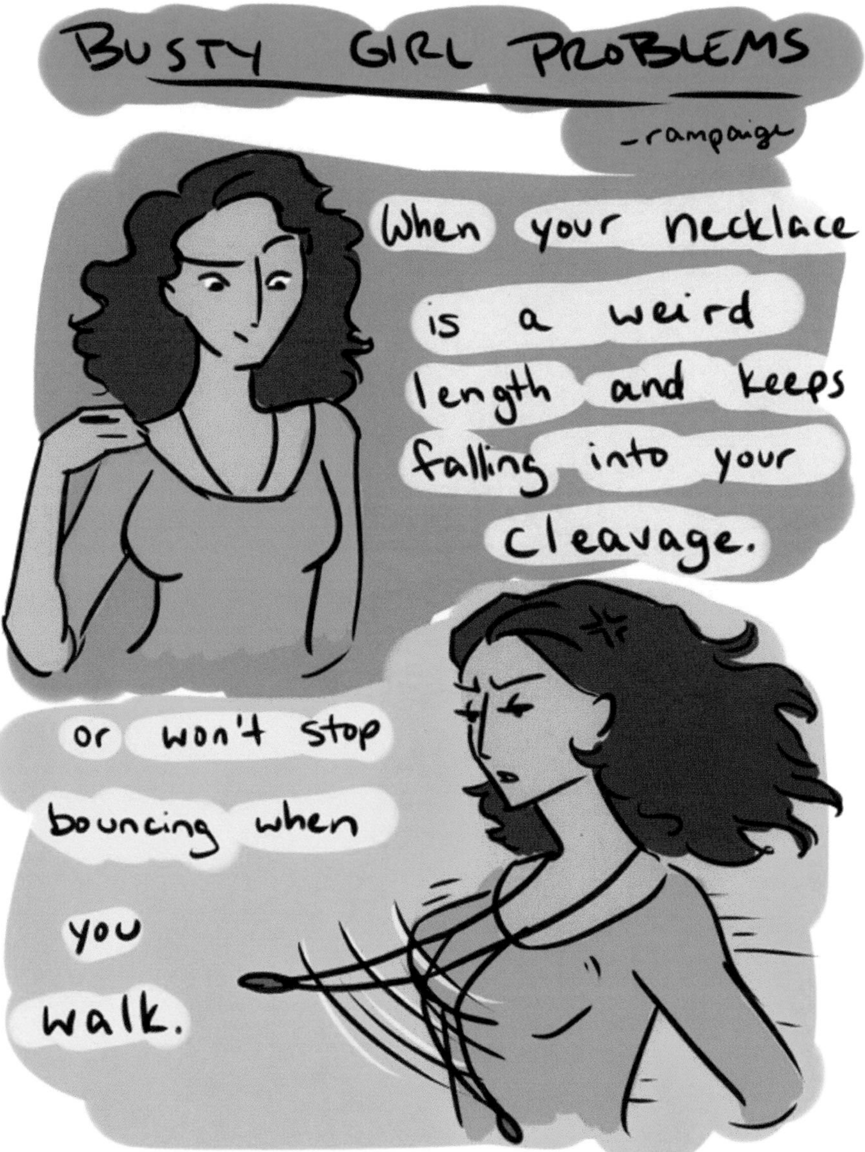
BUSTY GIRL PROBLEMS
-rampaige
When your necklace is a weird length and keeps falling into your cleavage.
or won't stop bouncing when you walk.

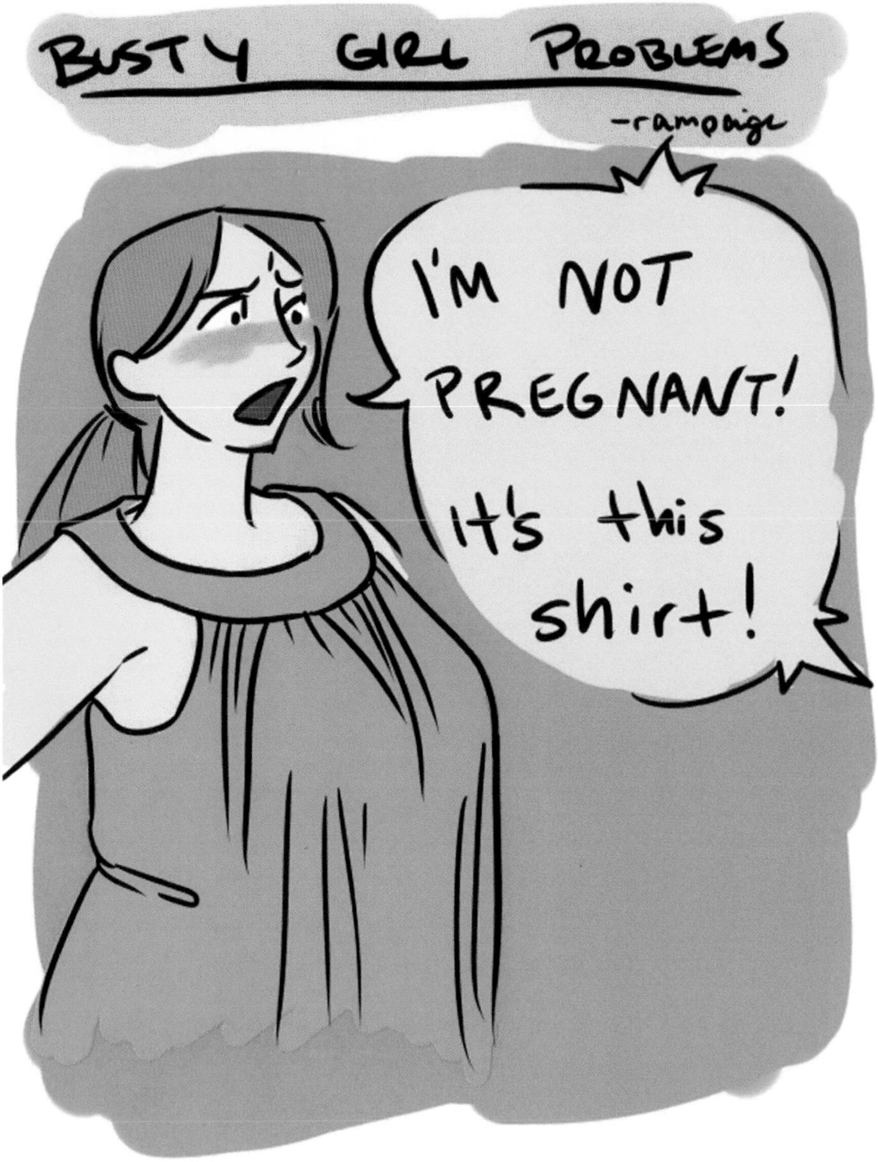
BUSTY GIRL PROBLEMS
-rampaige
I'M NOT PREGNANT! It's this shirt!

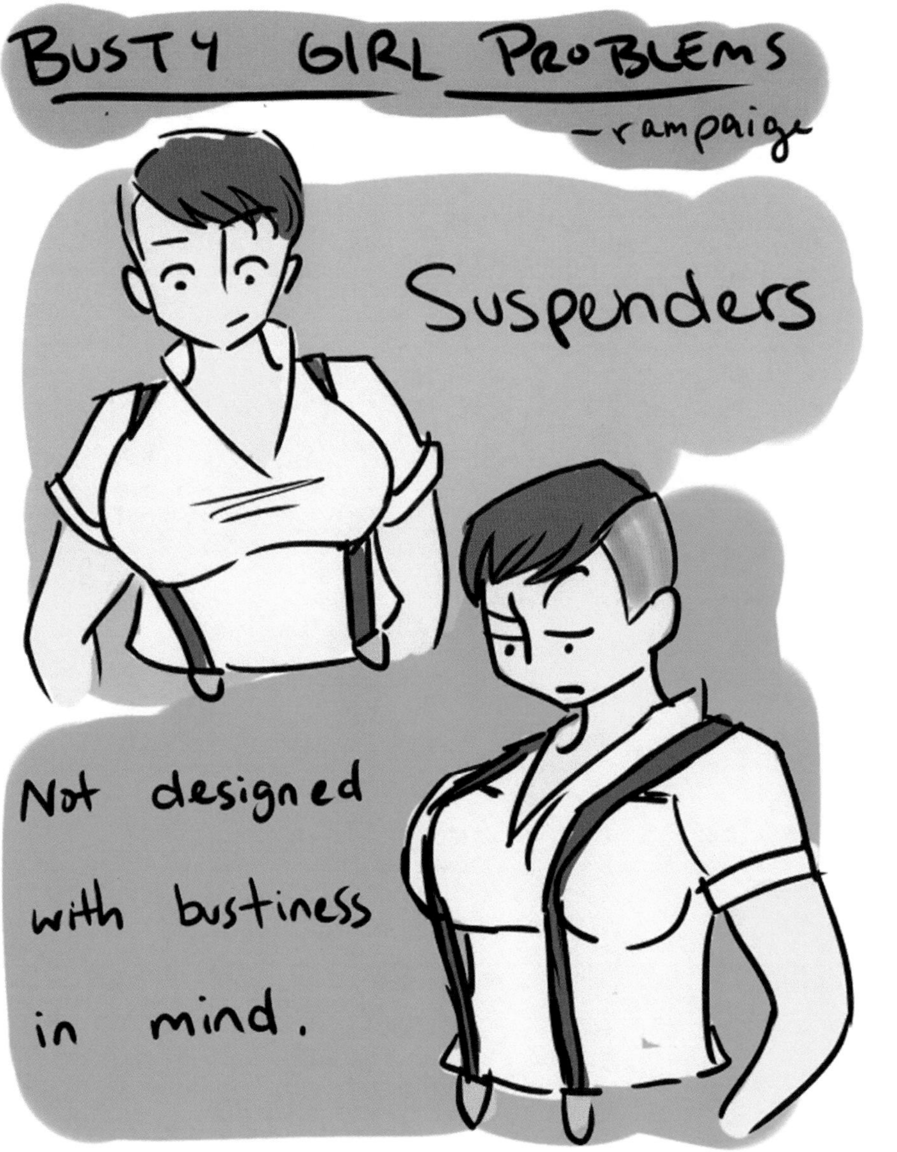
BUSTY GIRL PROBLEMS
-rampaige
Suspenders
Not designed with bustiness in mind.

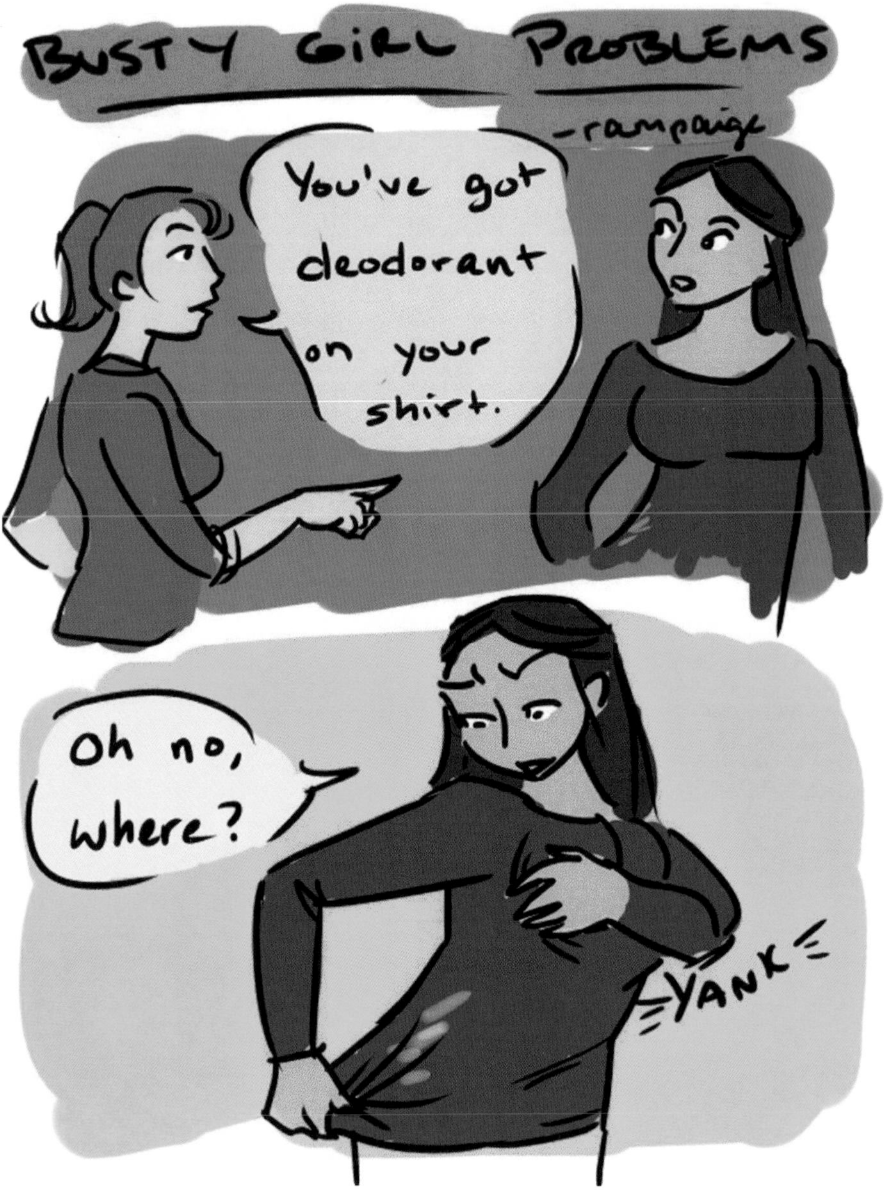
BUSTY GIRL PROBLEMS
-rampaige
You've got deodorant on your shirt.
Oh no, where?
YANK

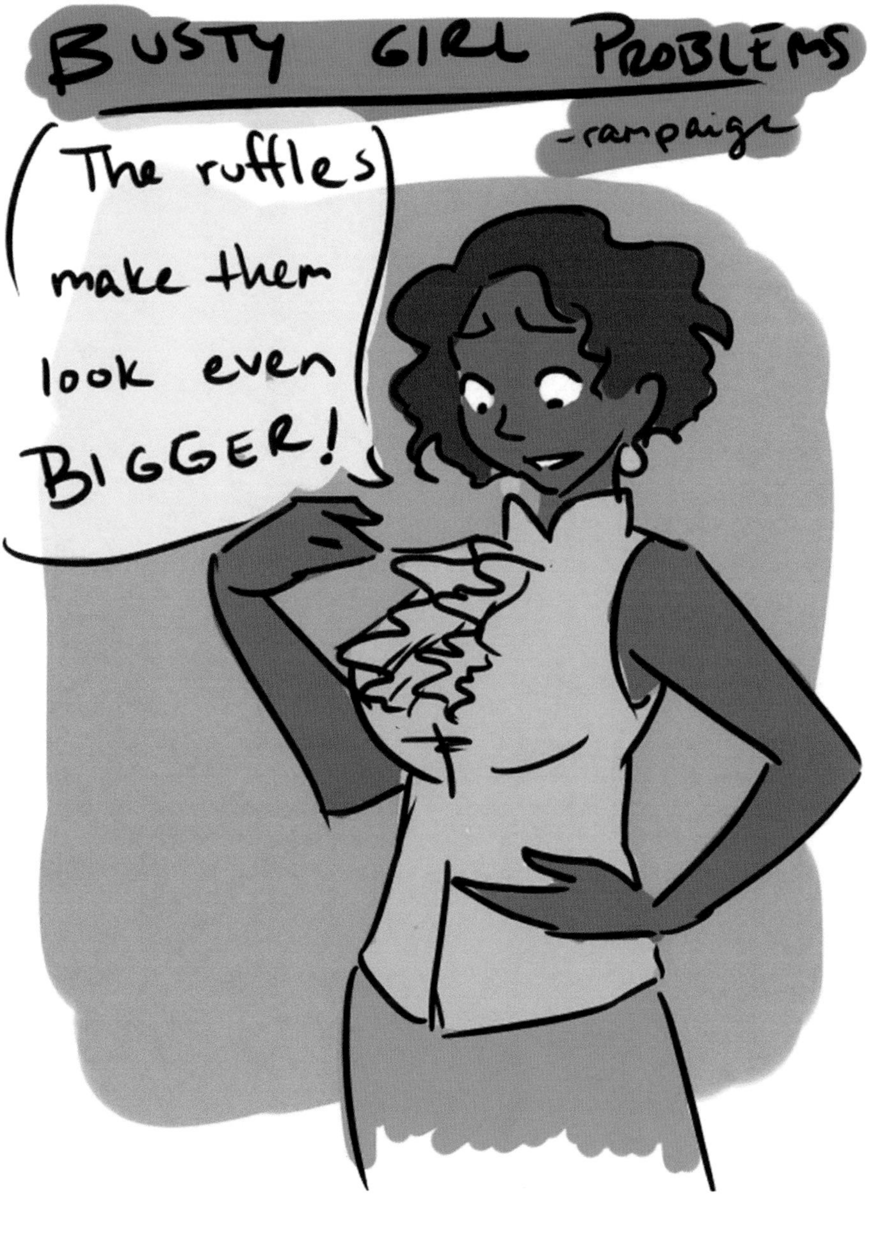
BUSTY GIRL PROBLEMS
-rampaige
The ruffles make them look even BIGGER!

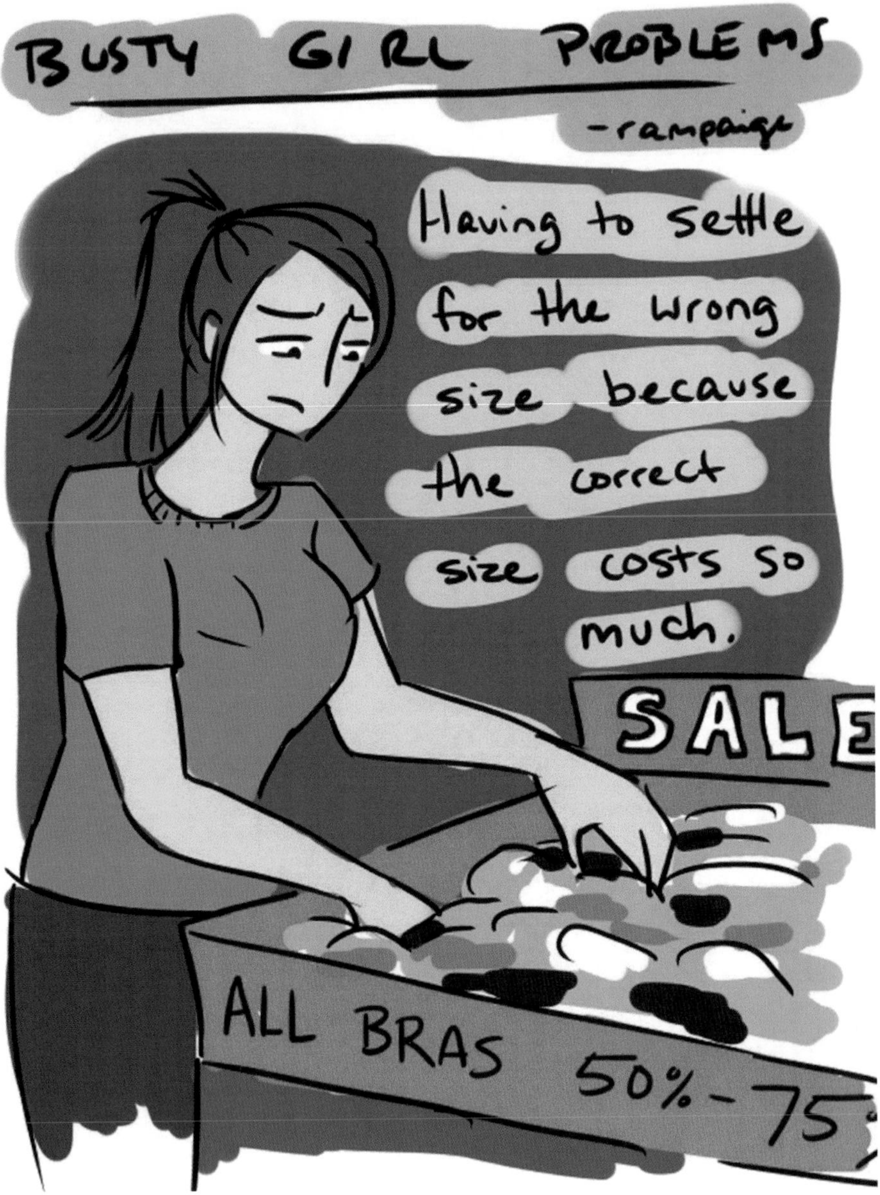
BUSTY GIRL PROBLEMS
-rampaige
Having to settle for the wrong size because the correct size costs so much.
SALE
ALL BRAS 50%-75

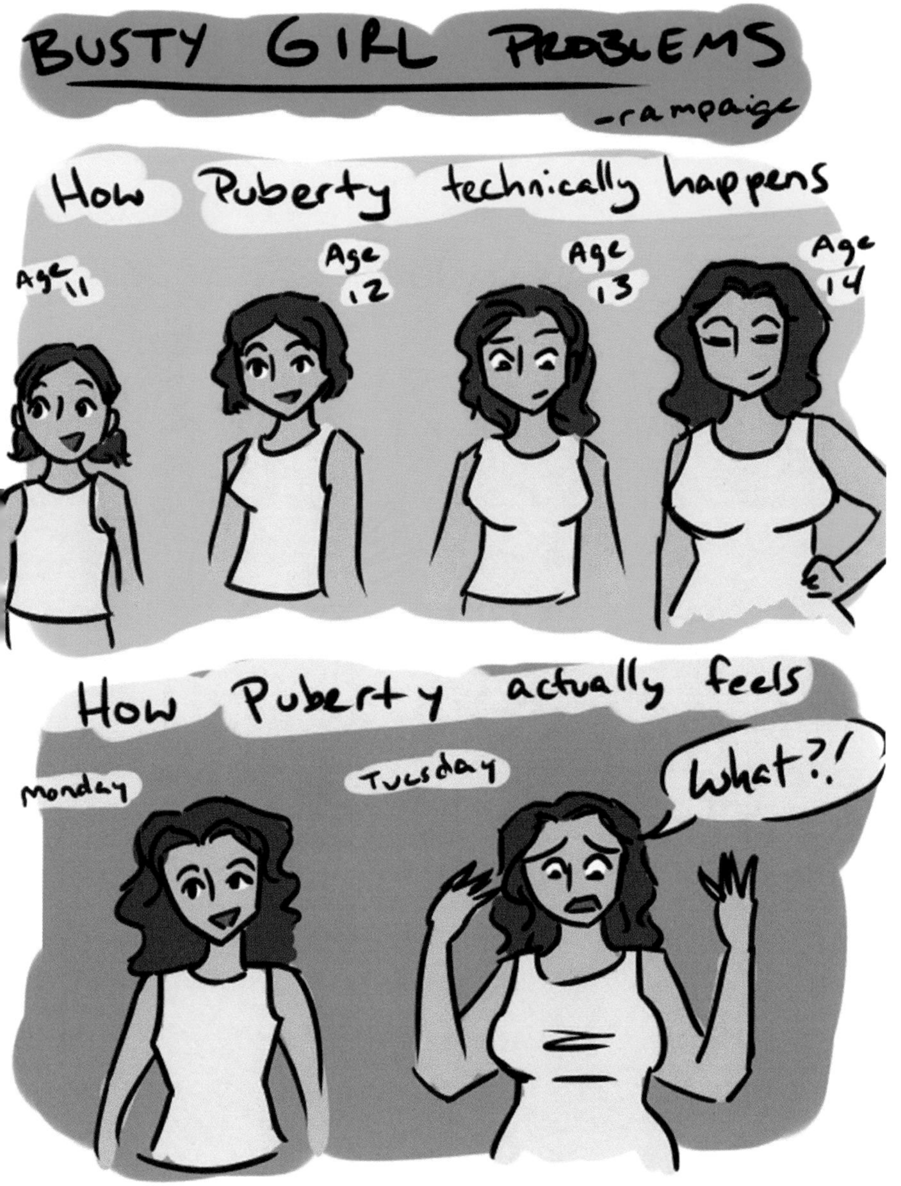
BUSTY GIRL PROBLEMS
-rampaige
How Puberty technically happens
Age 11
Age 12
Age 13
Age 14
How Puberty actually feels
Monday
Tuesday
What?!

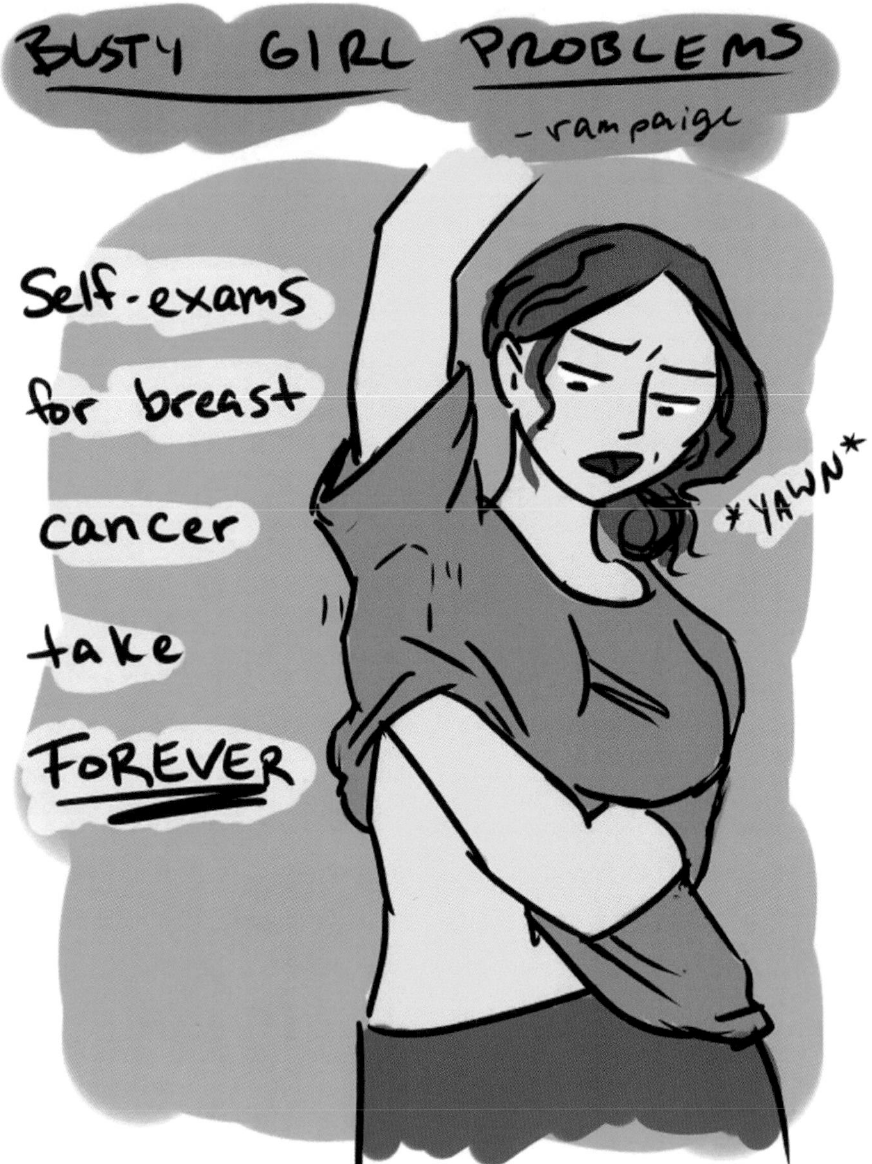
BUSTY GIRL PROBLEMS
-rampaige
Self-exams for breast cancer take FOREVER
YAWN

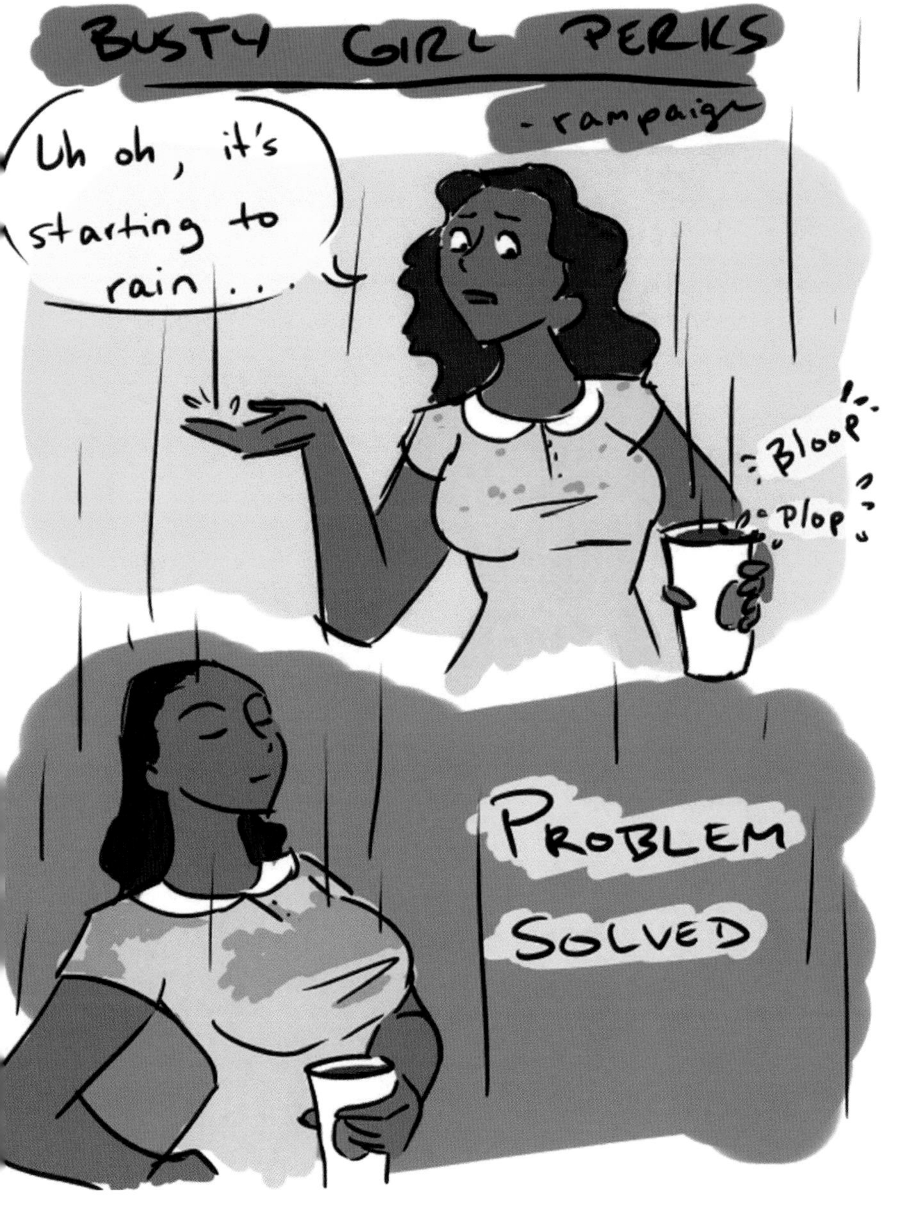

BUSTY GIRL PERKS
- rampaign
Uh oh, it's starting to rain...
Bloop
Plop
PROBLEM SOLVED

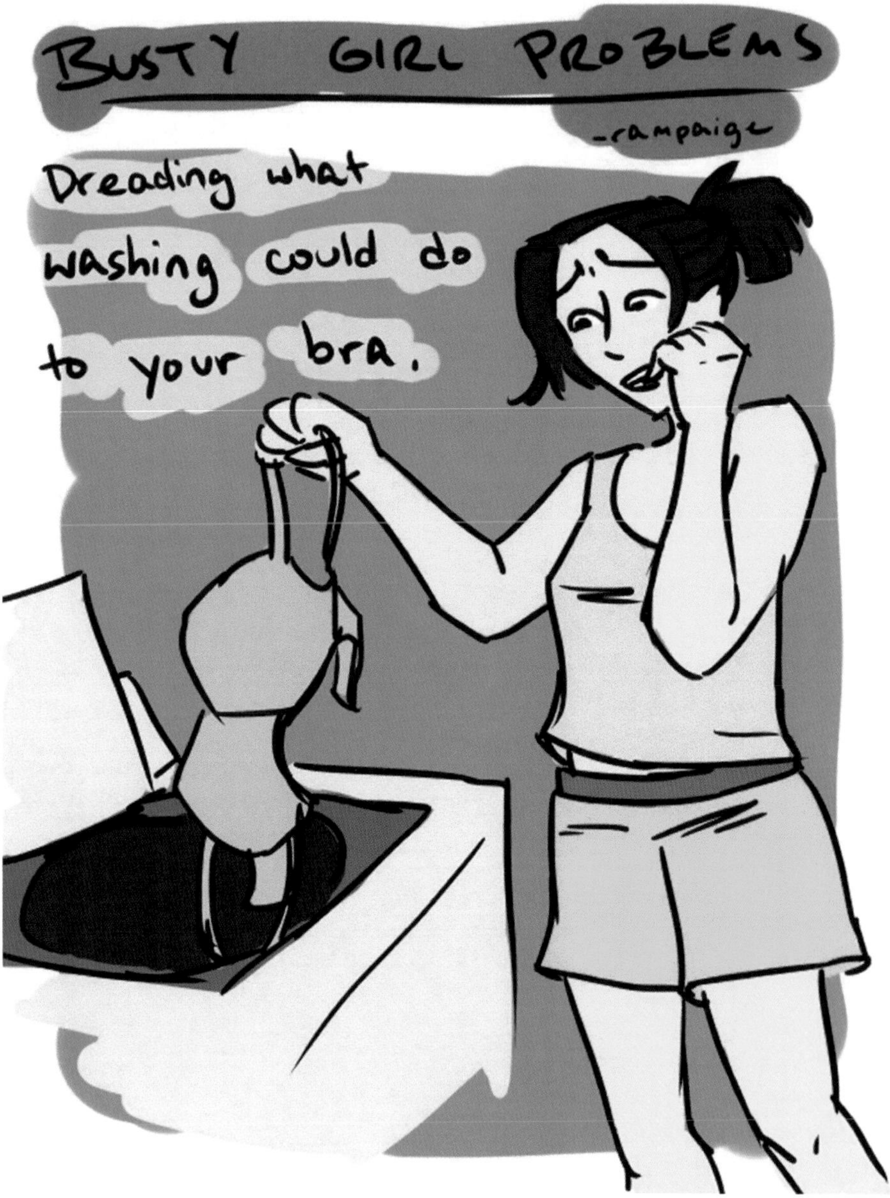
BUSTY GIRL PROBLEMS
-rampaige
Dreading what washing could do to your bra.

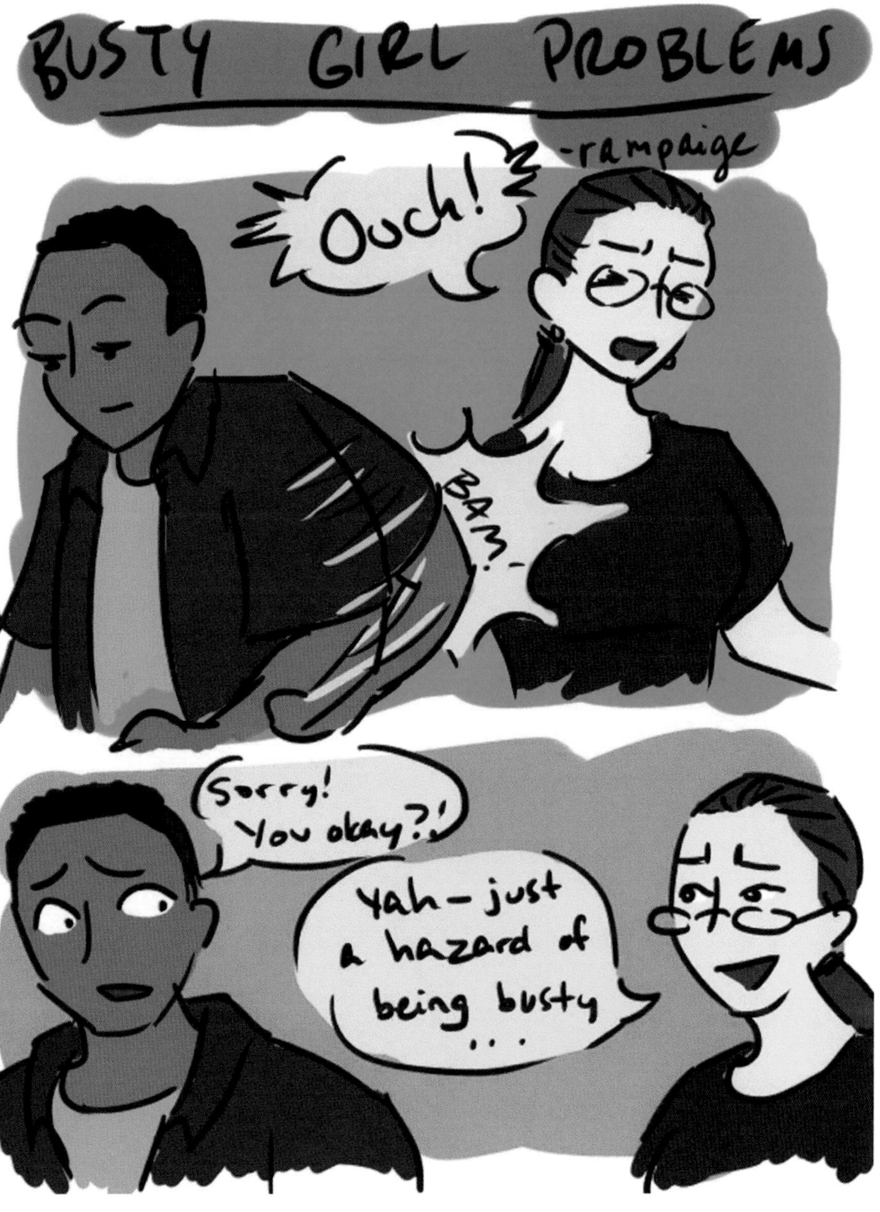
BUSTY GIRL PROBLEMS
-rampaige
Ouch!
BAM
Sorry! You okay?!
Yah - just a hazard of being busty ...

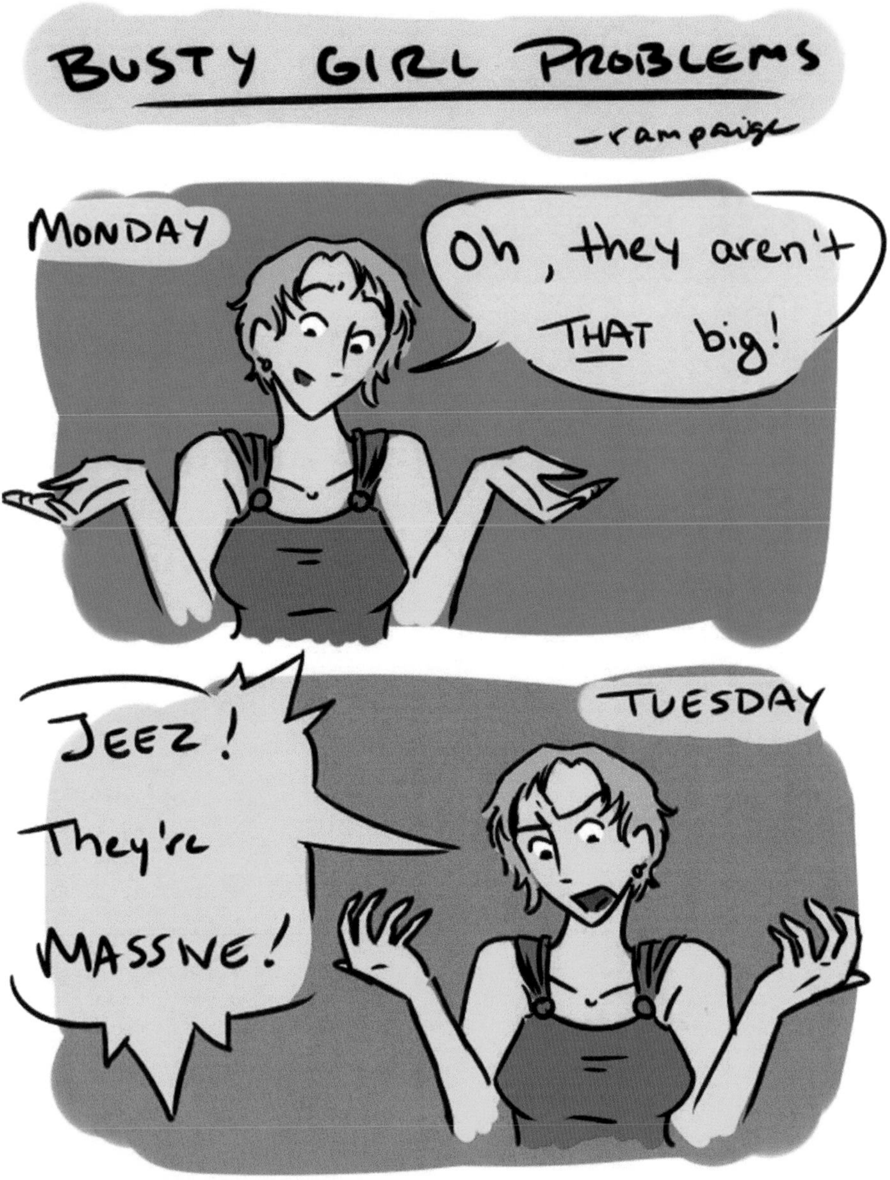
BUSTY GIRL PROBLEMS
-rampaige
MONDAY
Oh, they aren't THAT big!
TUESDAY
JEEZ! They're MASSIVE!

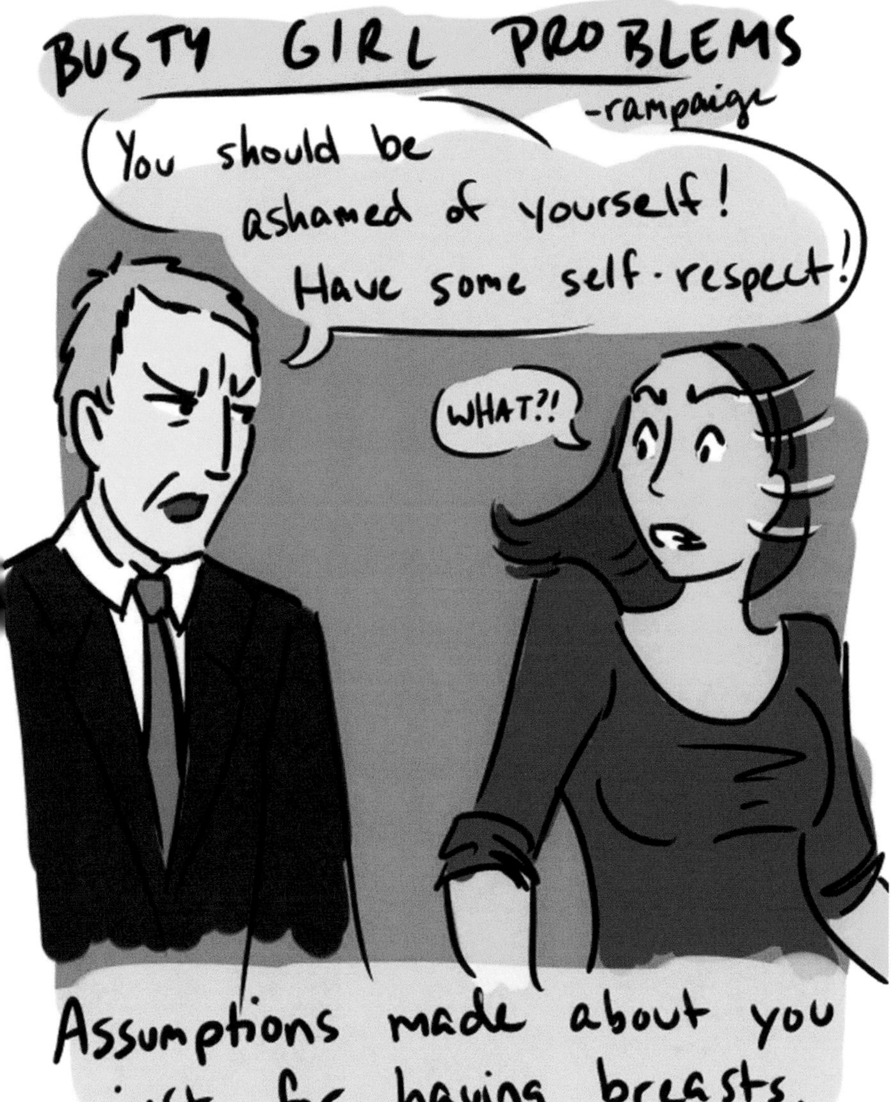
BUSTY GIRL PROBLEMS
-rampaige
You should be ashamed of yourself! Have some self-respect!
WHAT?!
Assumptions made about you just for having breasts.

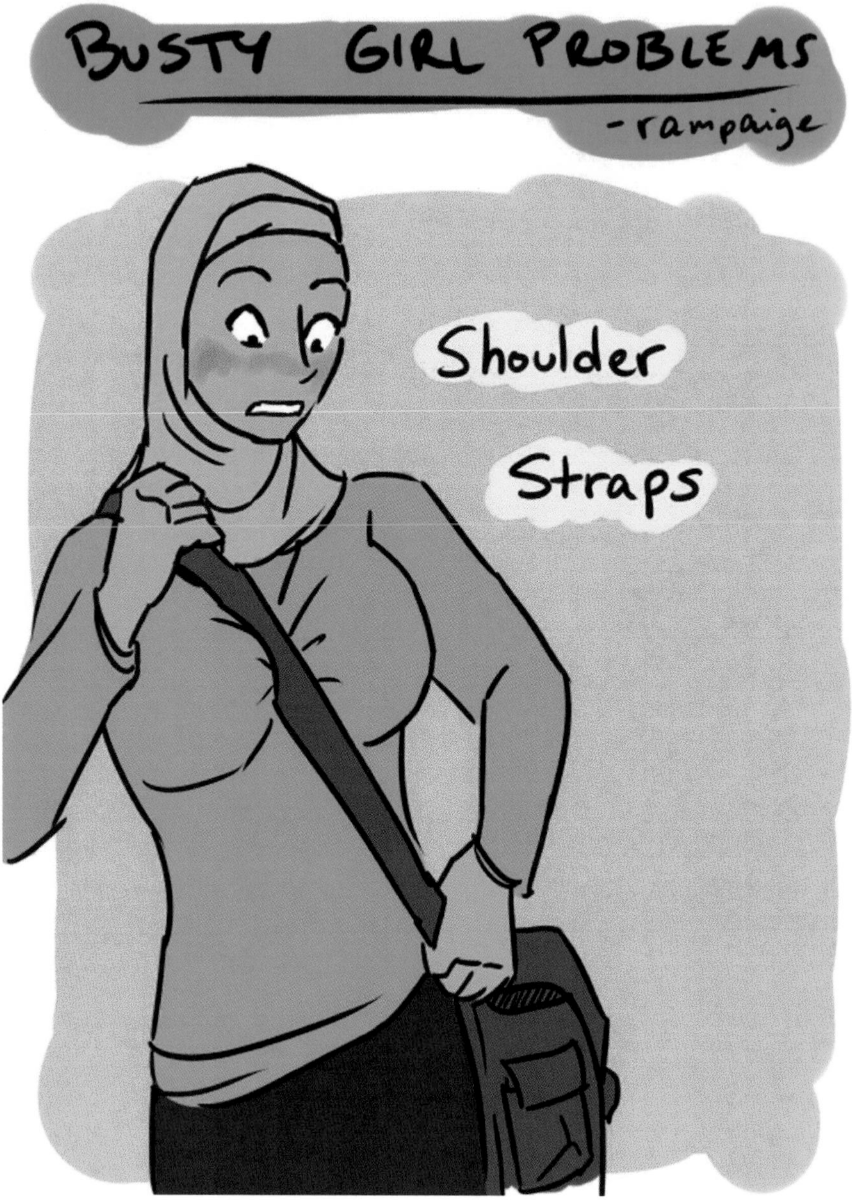
BUSTY GIRL PROBLEMS
-rampaige
Shoulder
Straps

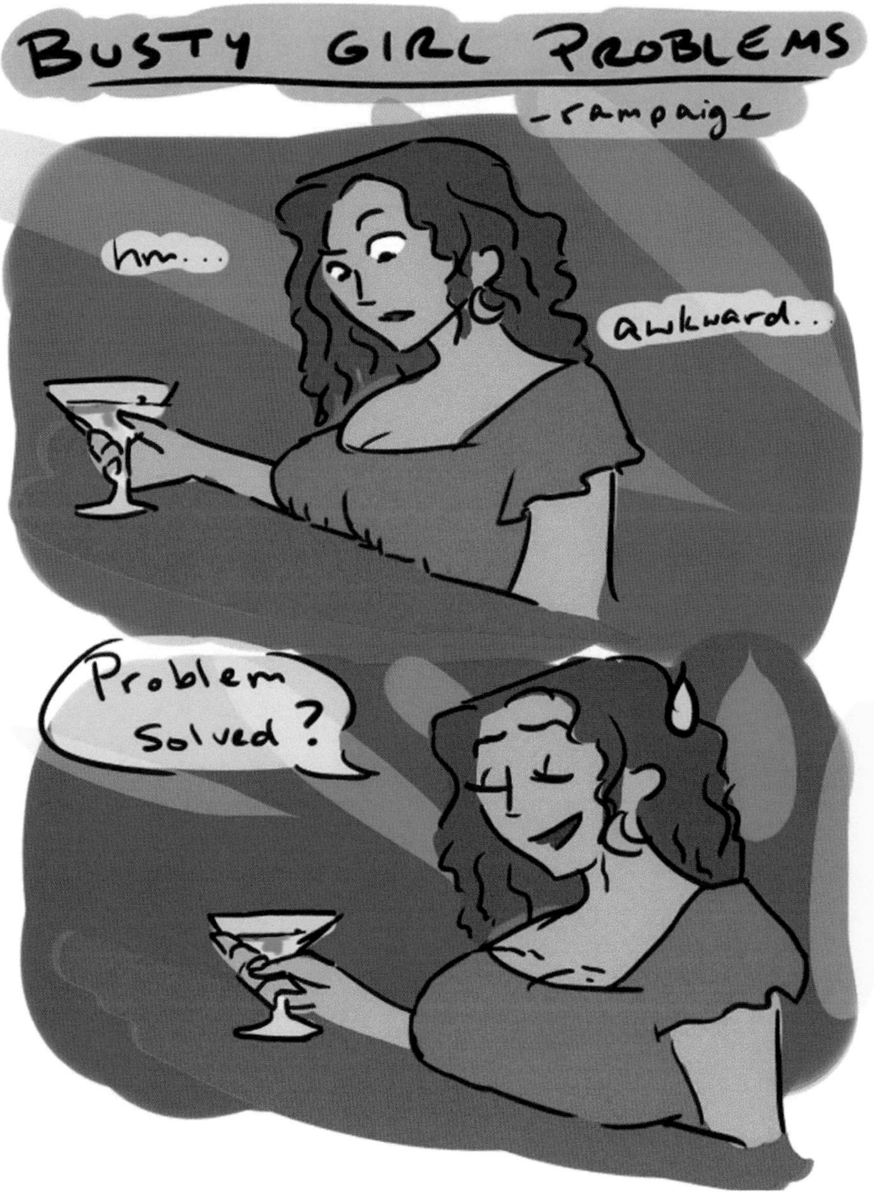
BUSTY GIRL PROBLEMS
-rampaige
hm...
awkward...
Problem solved?

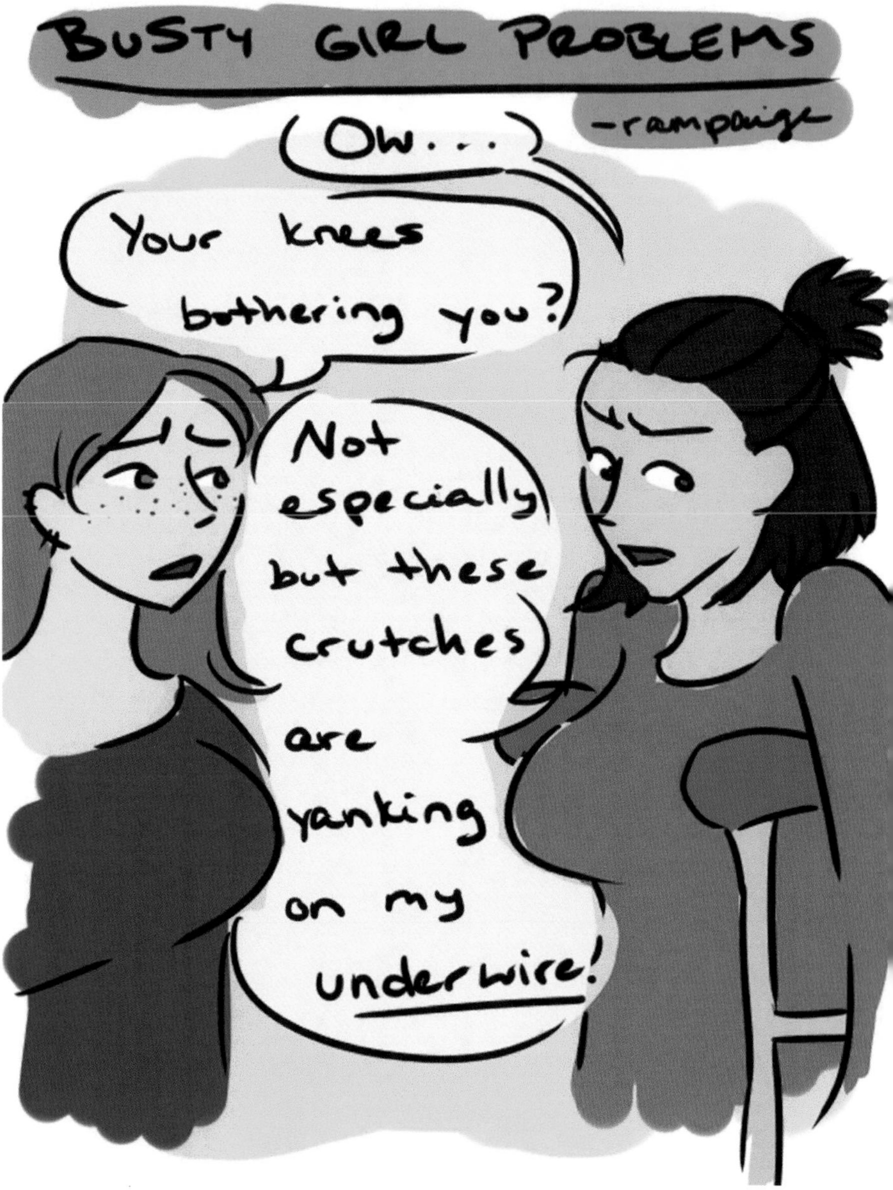
BUSTY GIRL PROBLEMS
-rampaige
Ow...
Your knees bothering you?
Not especially but these crutches are yanking on my underwire!

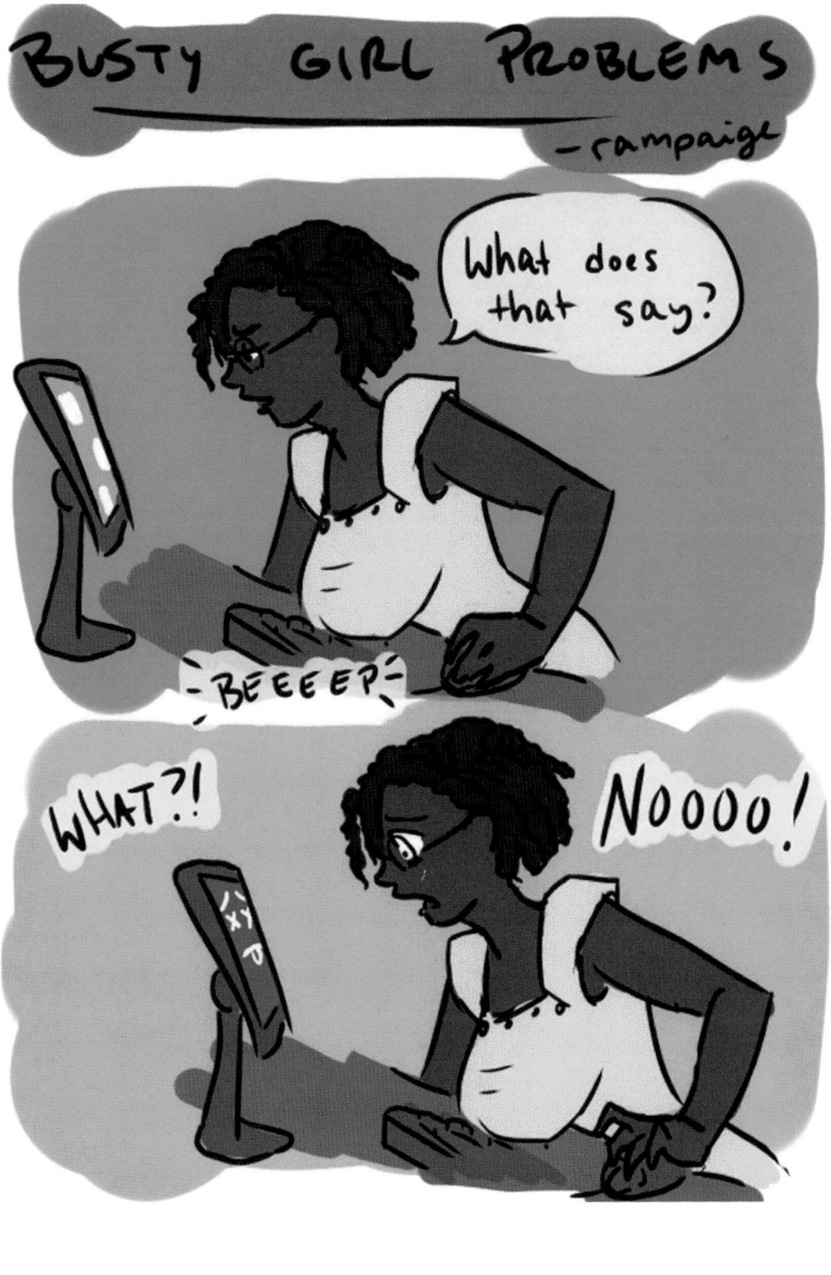
BUSTY GIRL PROBLEMS
-rampaige
What does that say?
-BEEEEP-
WHAT?!
NOOOO!

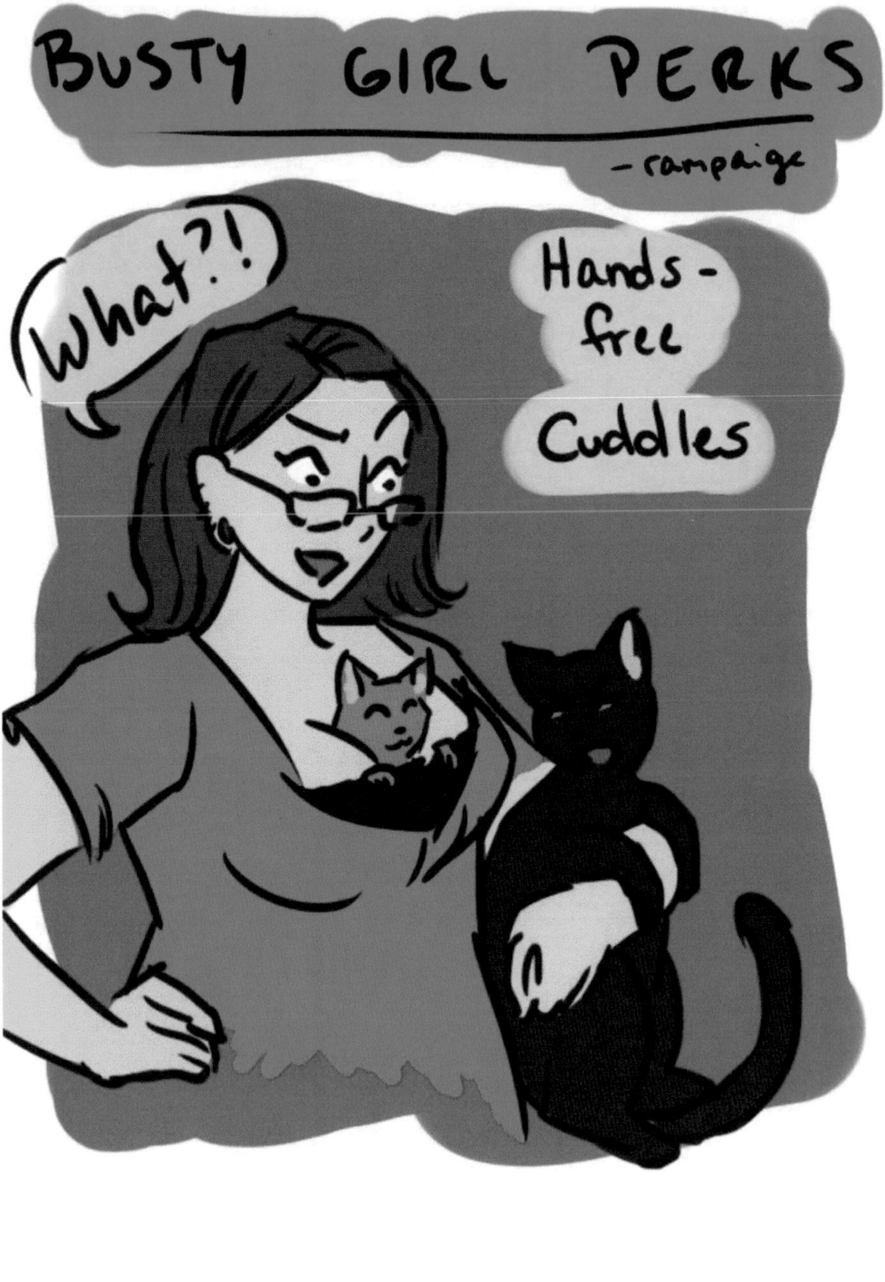
BUSTY GIRL PERKS
-rampaige
What?!
Hands-free Cuddles

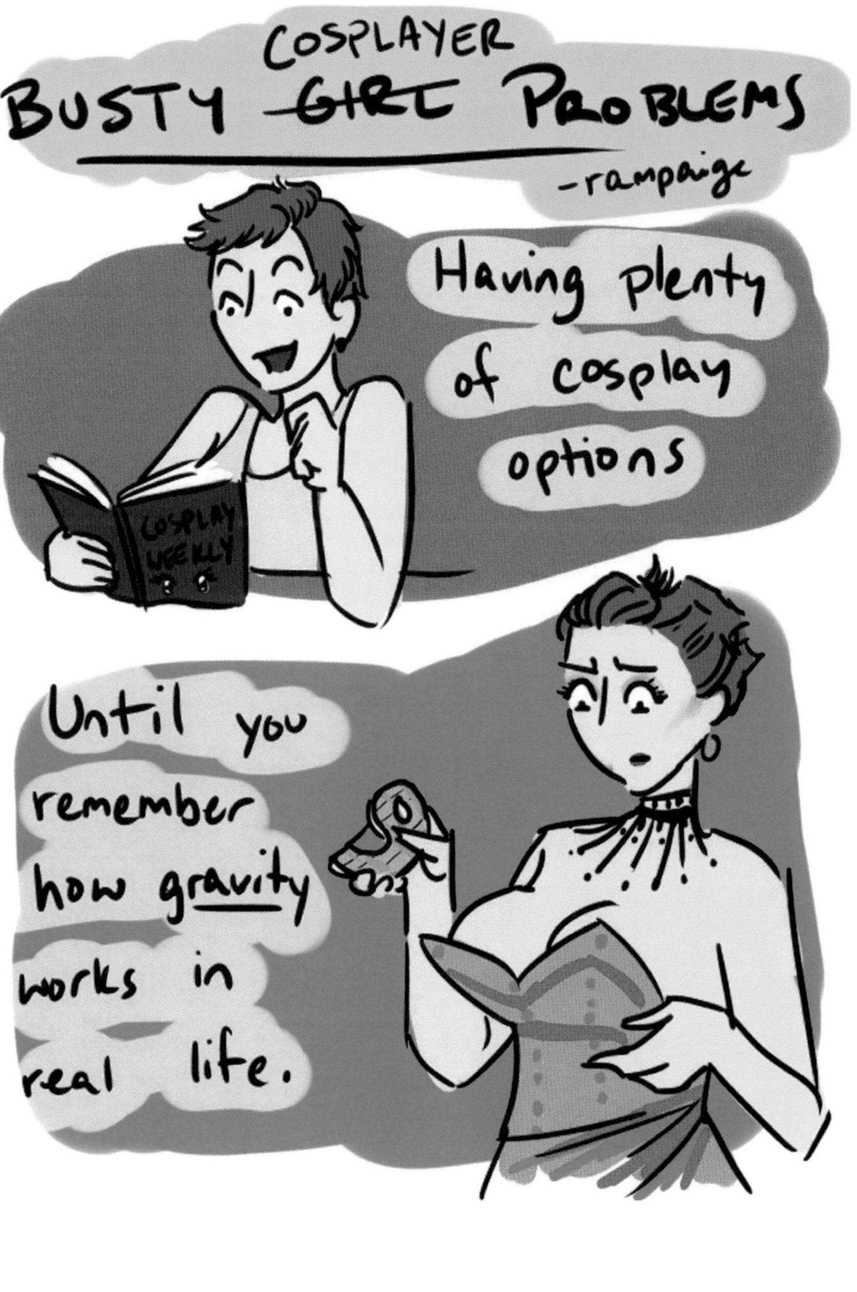
COSPLAYER
BUSTY GIRL PROBLEMS
-rampaige
Having plenty of cosplay options
COSPLAY WEEKLY
Until you remember how gravity works in real life.

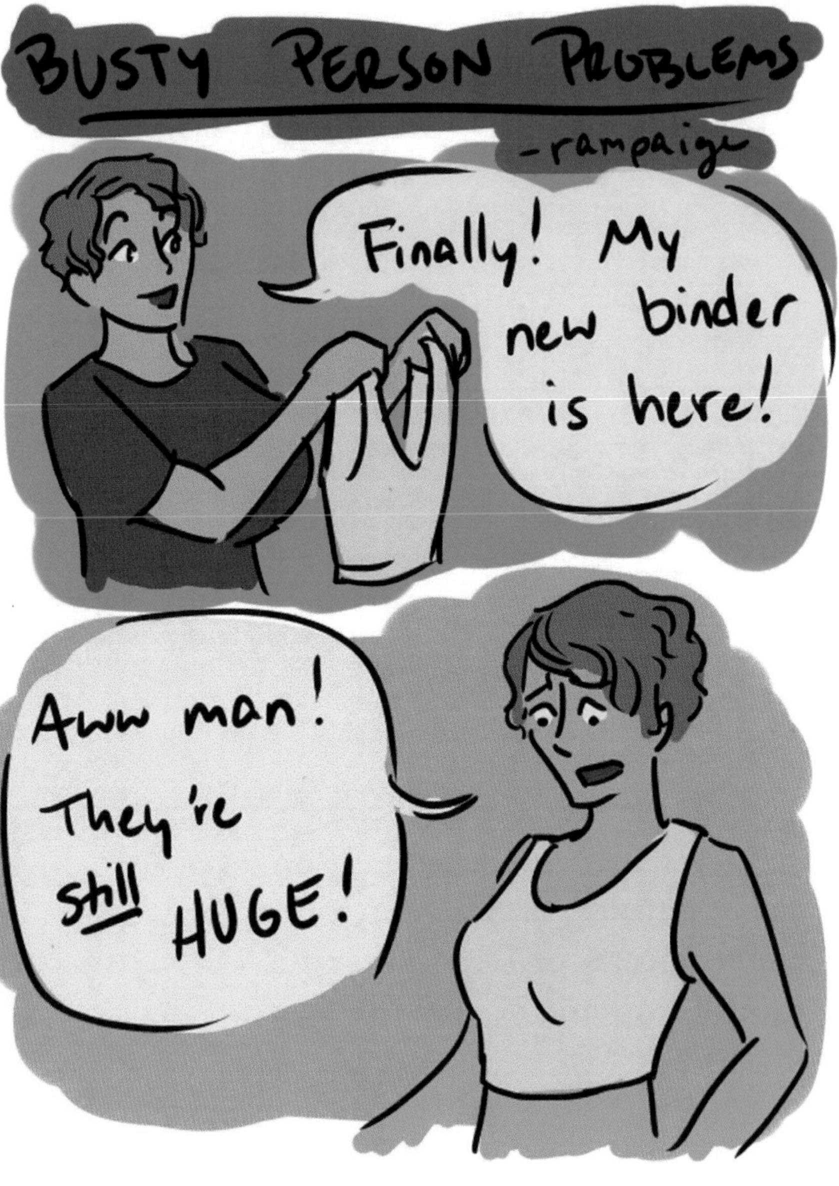
BUSTY PERSON PROBLEMS
-rampaige
Finally! My new binder is here!
Aww man! They're still HUGE!

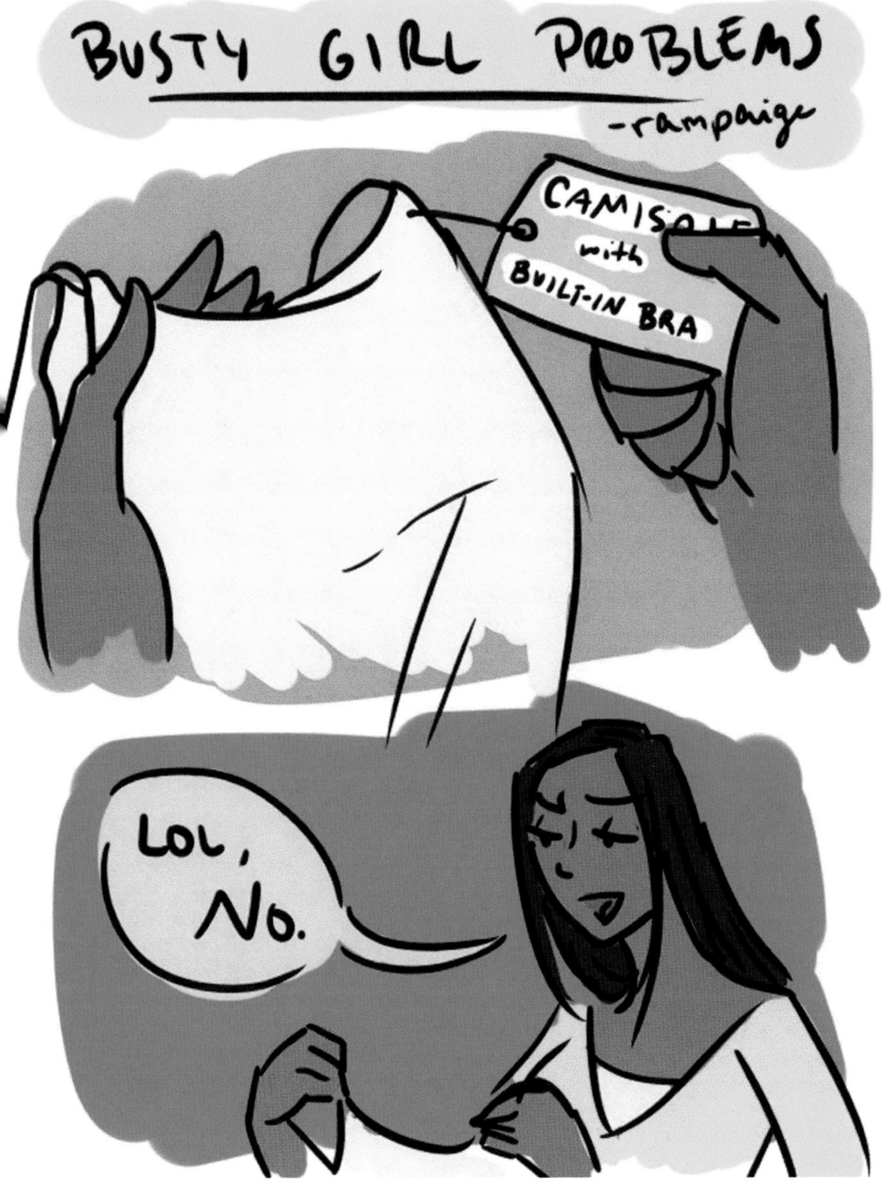
BUSTY GIRL PROBLEMS
-rampaige
CAMISO
with
BUILT-IN BRA
LOL, NO.

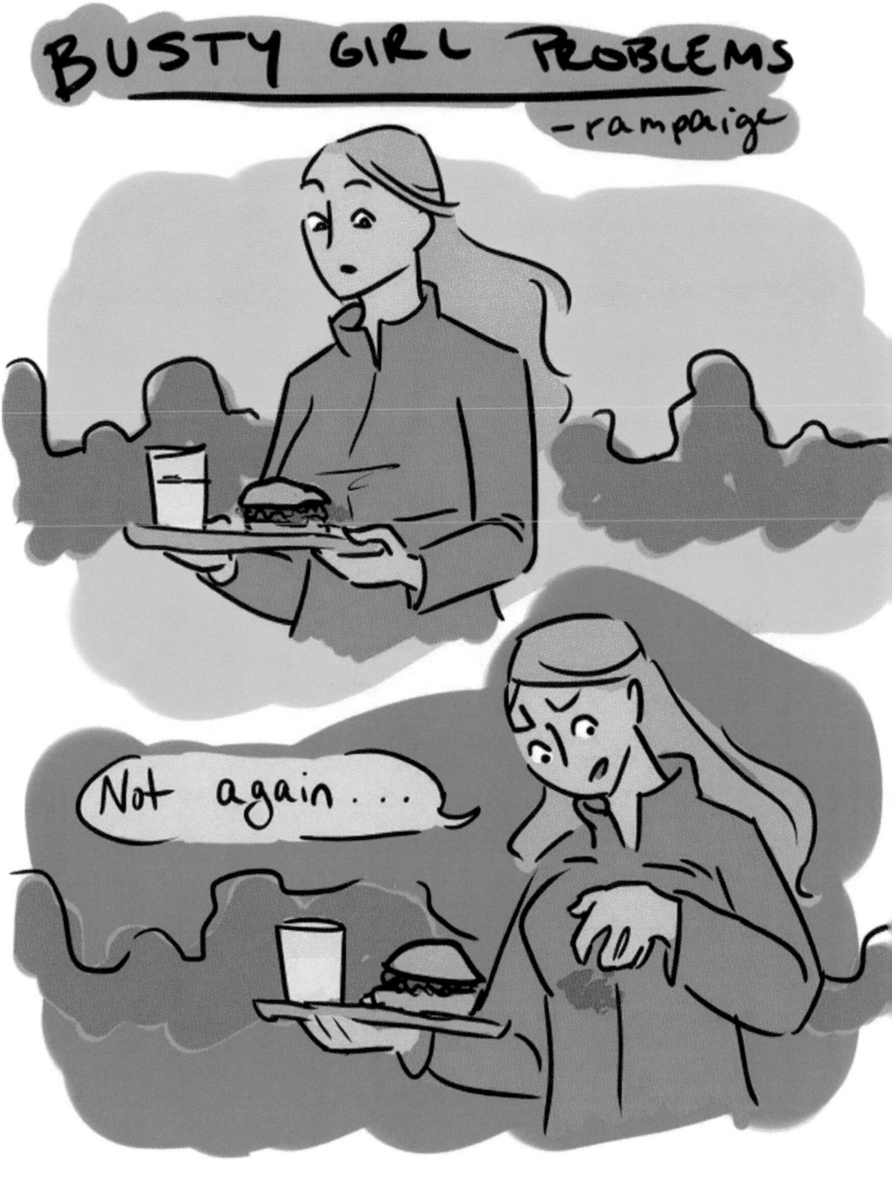
BUSTY GIRL PROBLEMS
-rampaige
Not again . . .

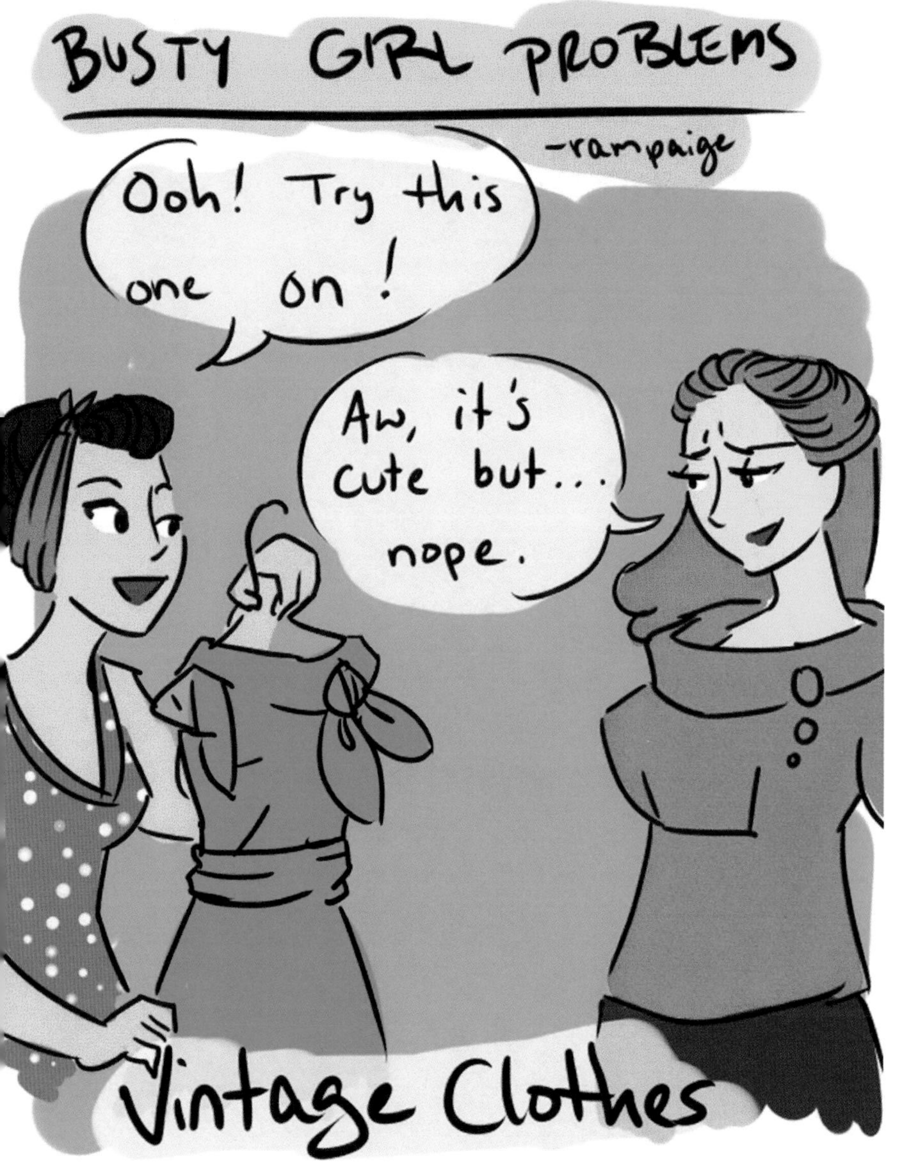
BUSTY GIRL PROBLEMS
-rampaige
Ooh! Try this one on!
Aw, it's cute but... nope.
Vintage Clothes

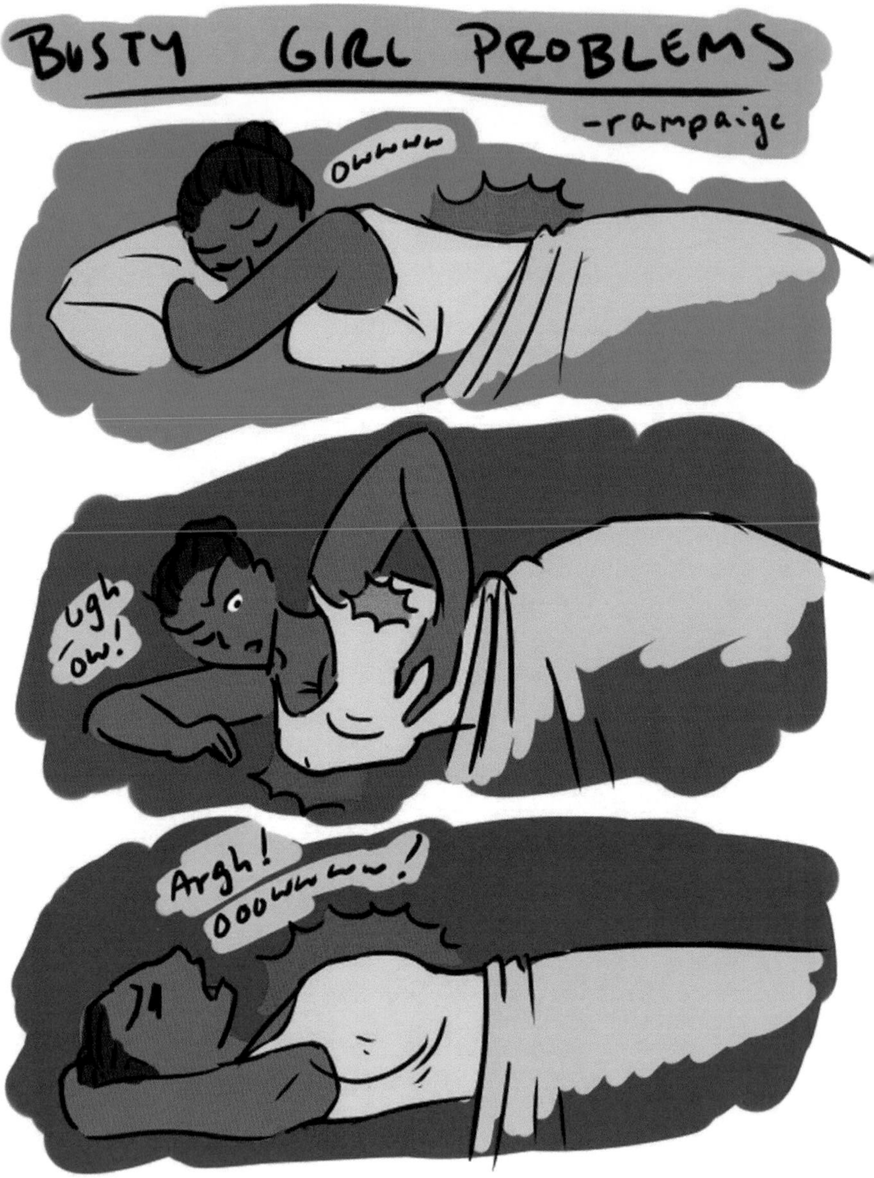
BUSTY GIRL PROBLEMS
-rampaige
OWWWW
Ugh ow!
Argh! OOOWWWWW!

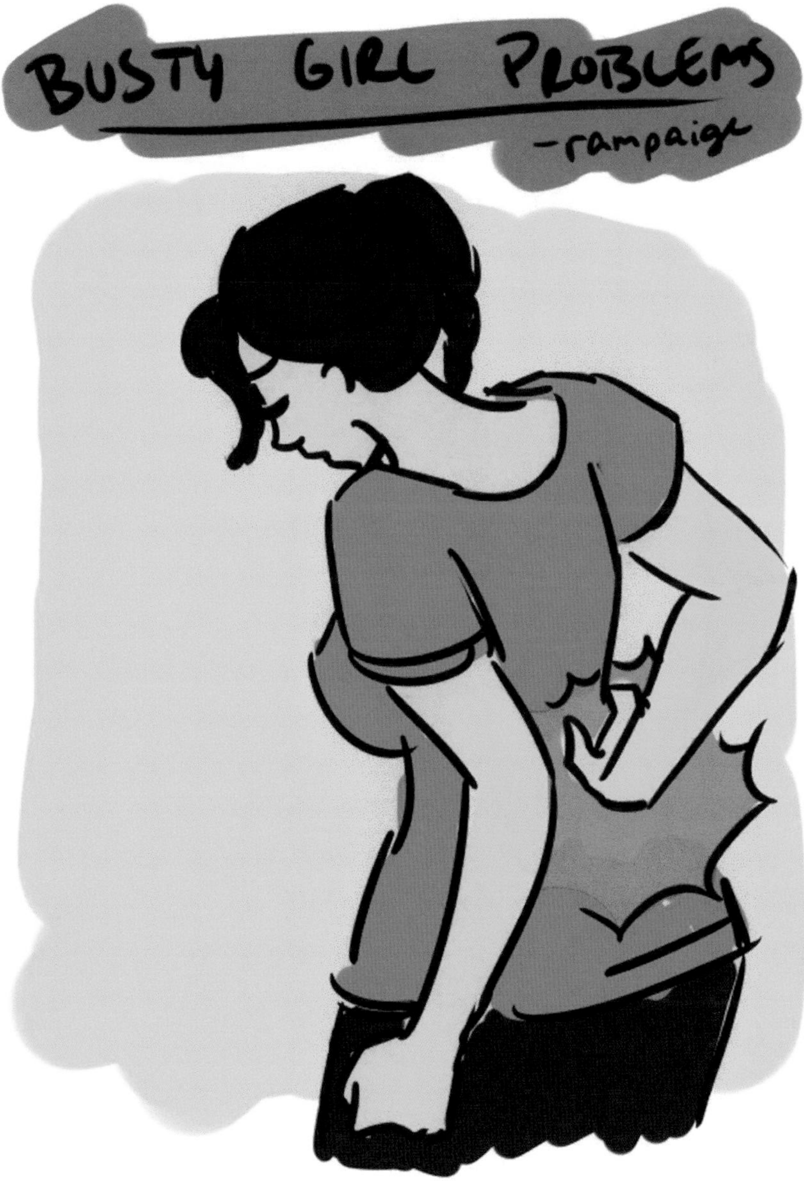
BUSTY GIRL PROBLEMS
-rampaige

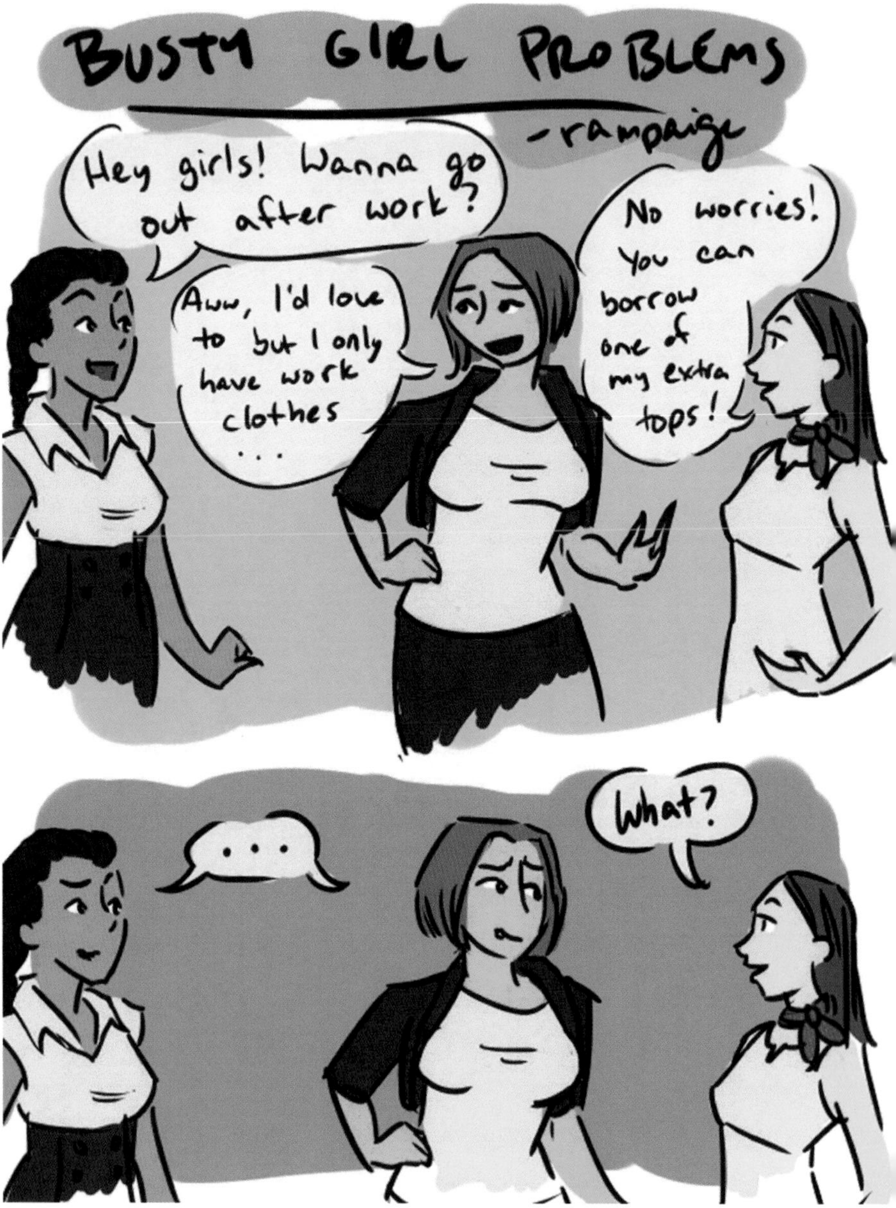
BUSTY GIRL PROBLEMS
-rampaige
Hey girls! Wanna go out after work?
Aww, I'd love to but I only have work clothes . . .
No worries! You can borrow one of my extra tops!
. . .
What?

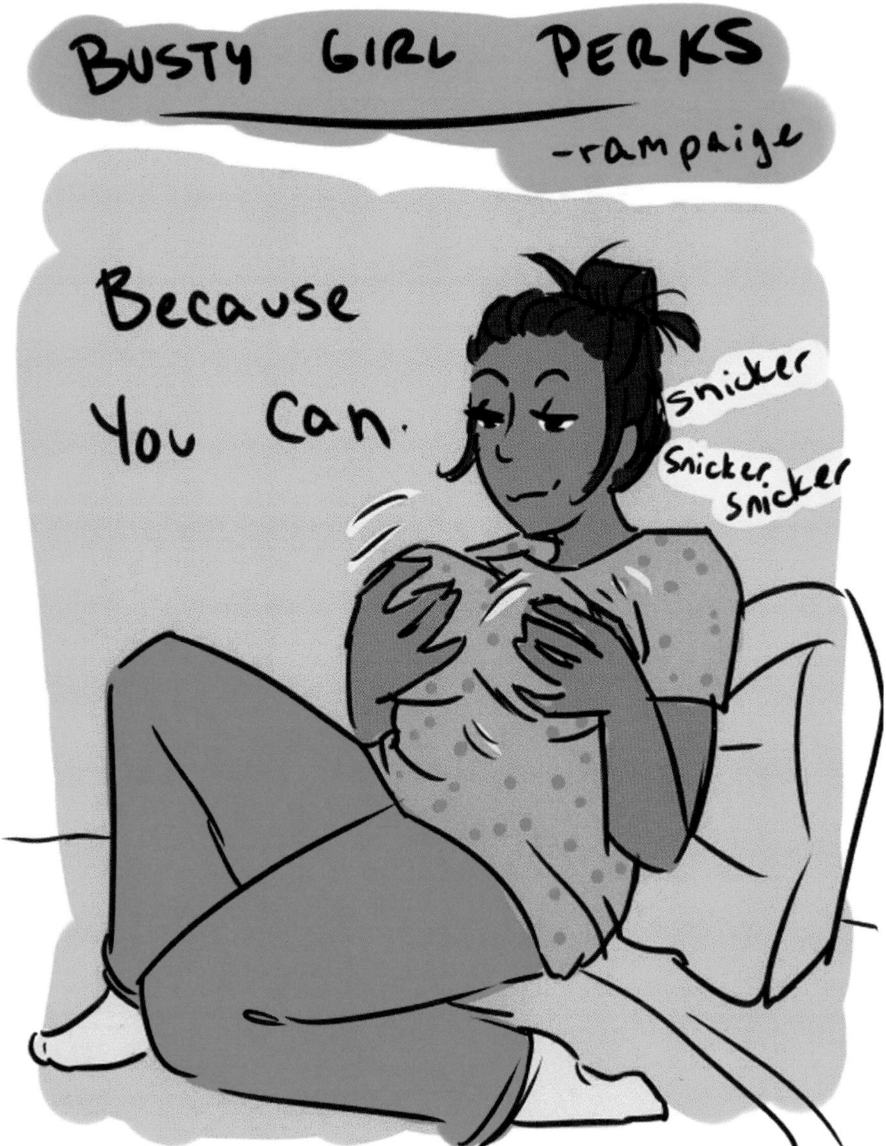
BUSTY GIRL PERKS
-rampaige
Because You can.
snicker
Snicker snicker

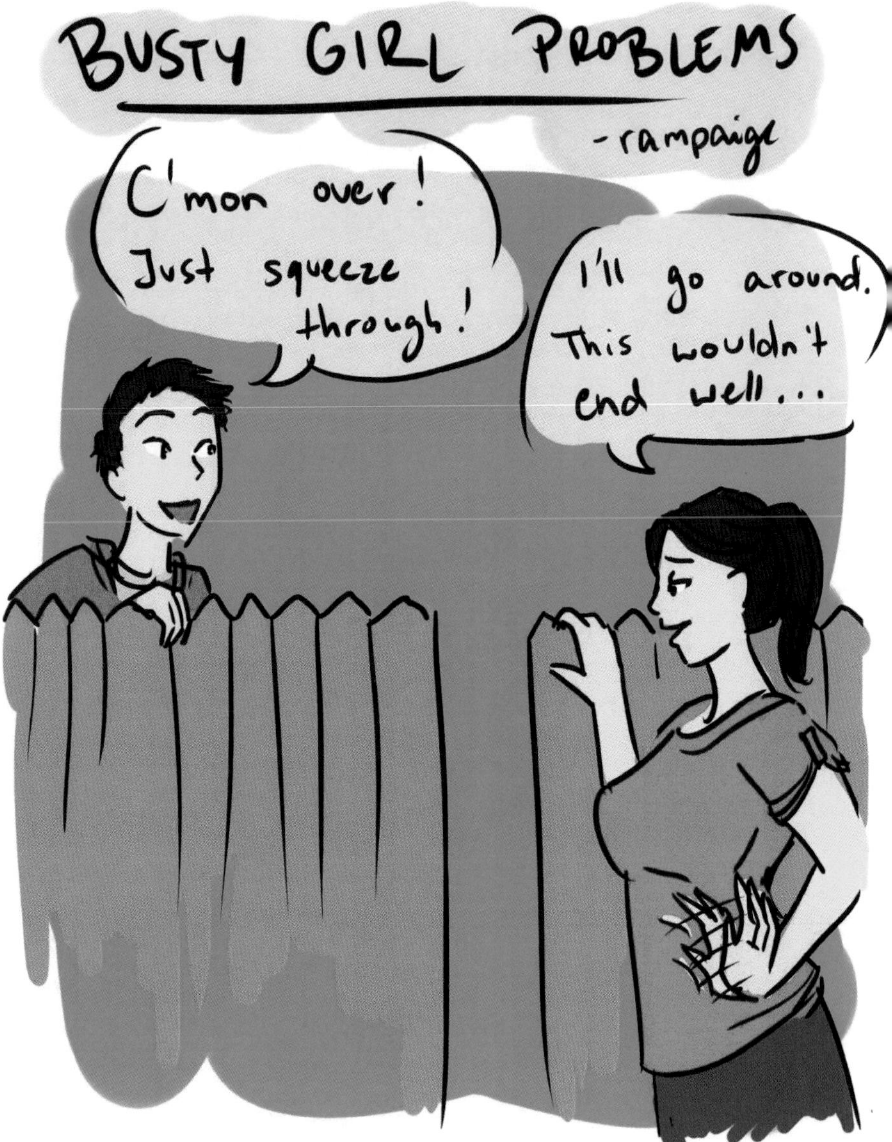
BUSTY GIRL PROBLEMS
-rampaige
C'mon over! Just squeeze through!
I'll go around. This wouldn't end well...

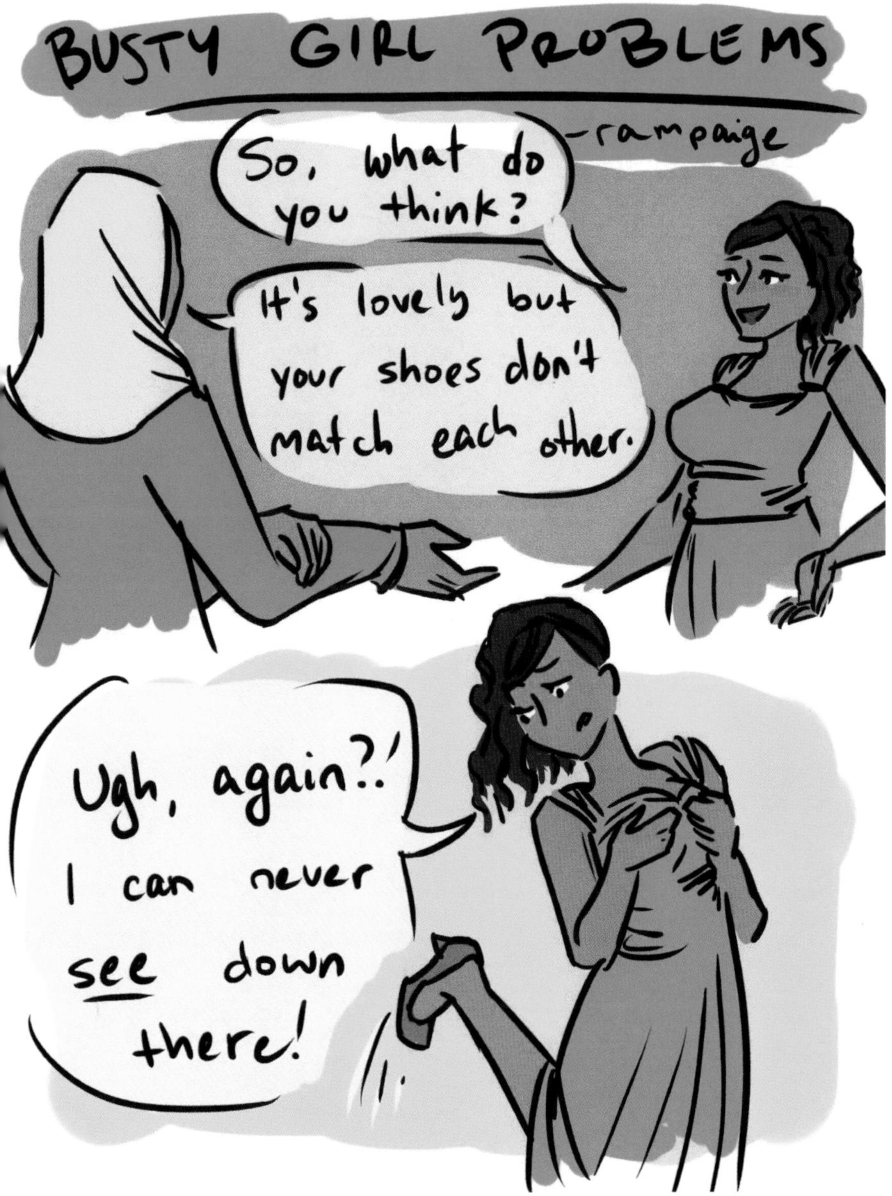
BUSTY GIRL PROBLEMS
-rampaige
So, what do you think?
It's lovely but your shoes don't match each other.
Ugh, again?! I can never see down there!

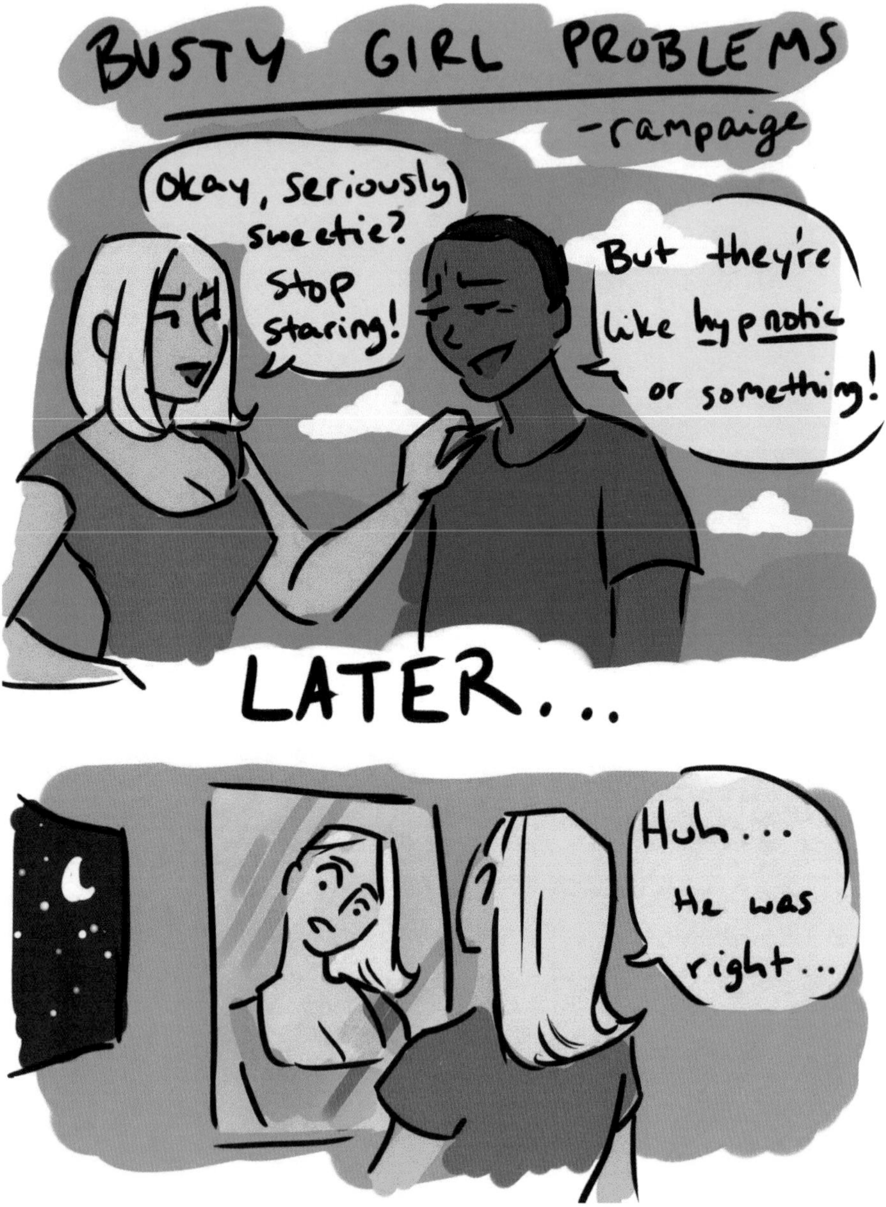
BUSTY GIRL PROBLEMS
-rampaige
Okay, seriously sweetie? Stop staring!
But they're like hypnotic or something!
LATER...
Huh... He was right...

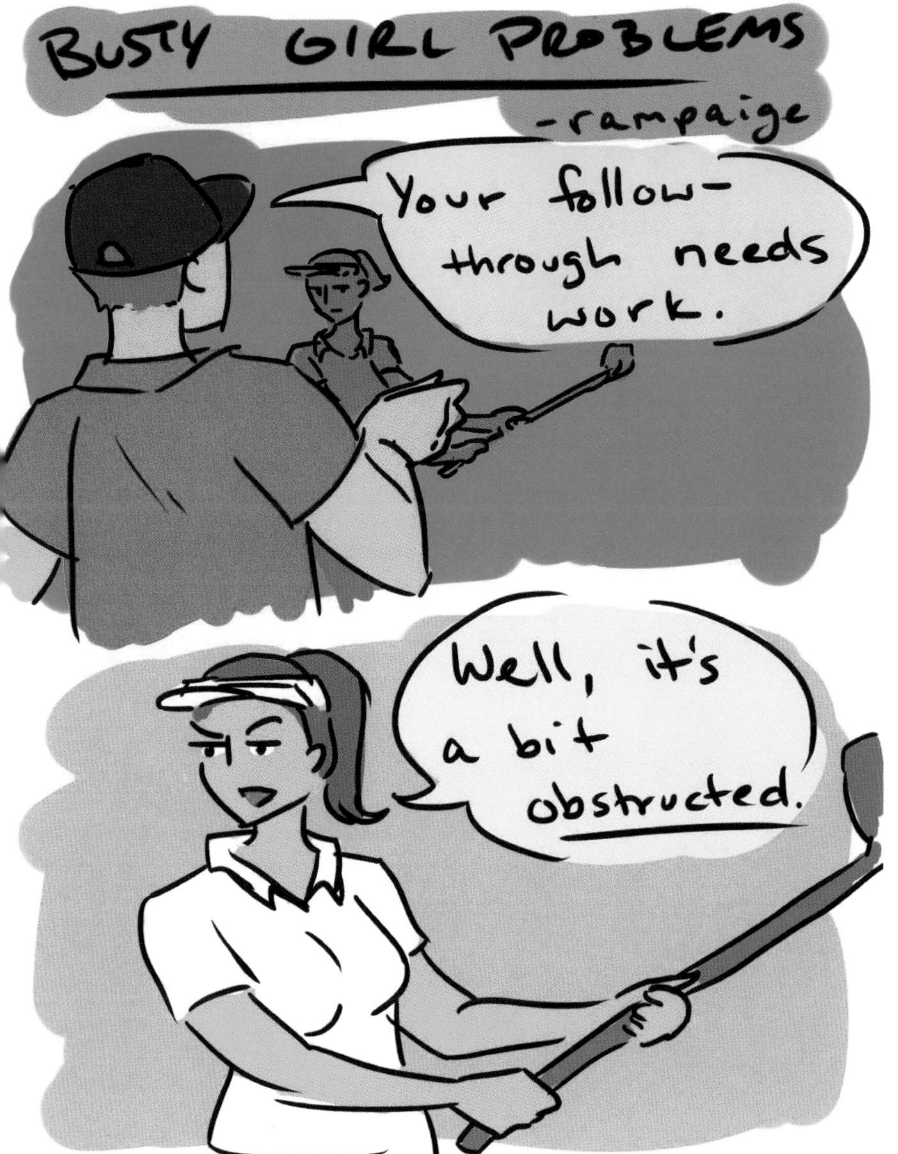
BUSTY GIRL PROBLEMS
-rampaige
Your follow-through needs work.
Well, it's a bit obstructed.

BUSTY GIRL PROBLEMS

-rampaige

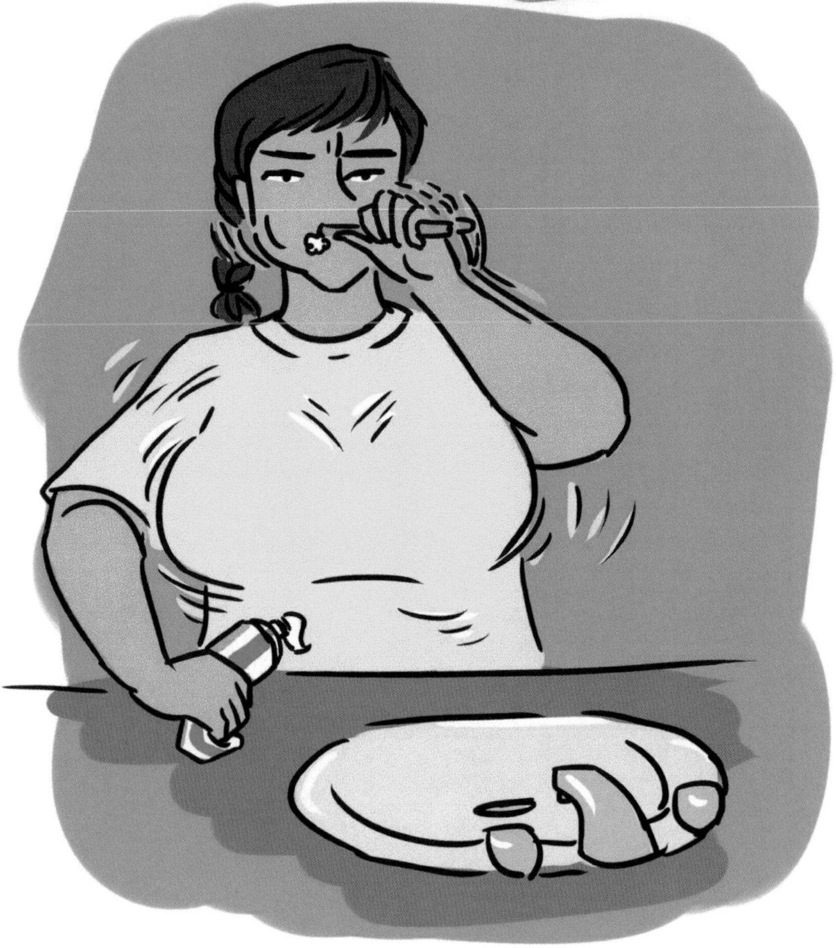

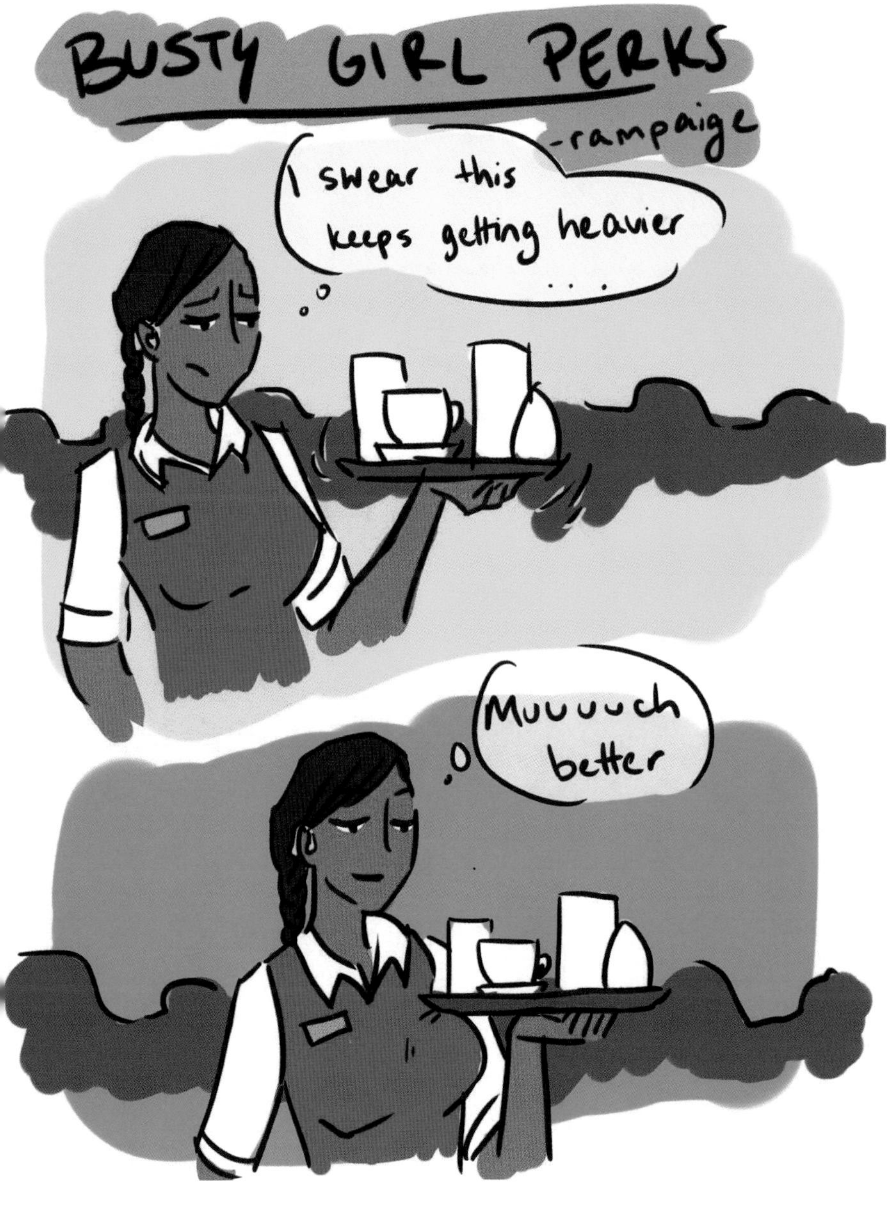
BUSTY GIRL PERKS
-rampaige
I swear this keeps getting heavier . . .
Muuuuch better

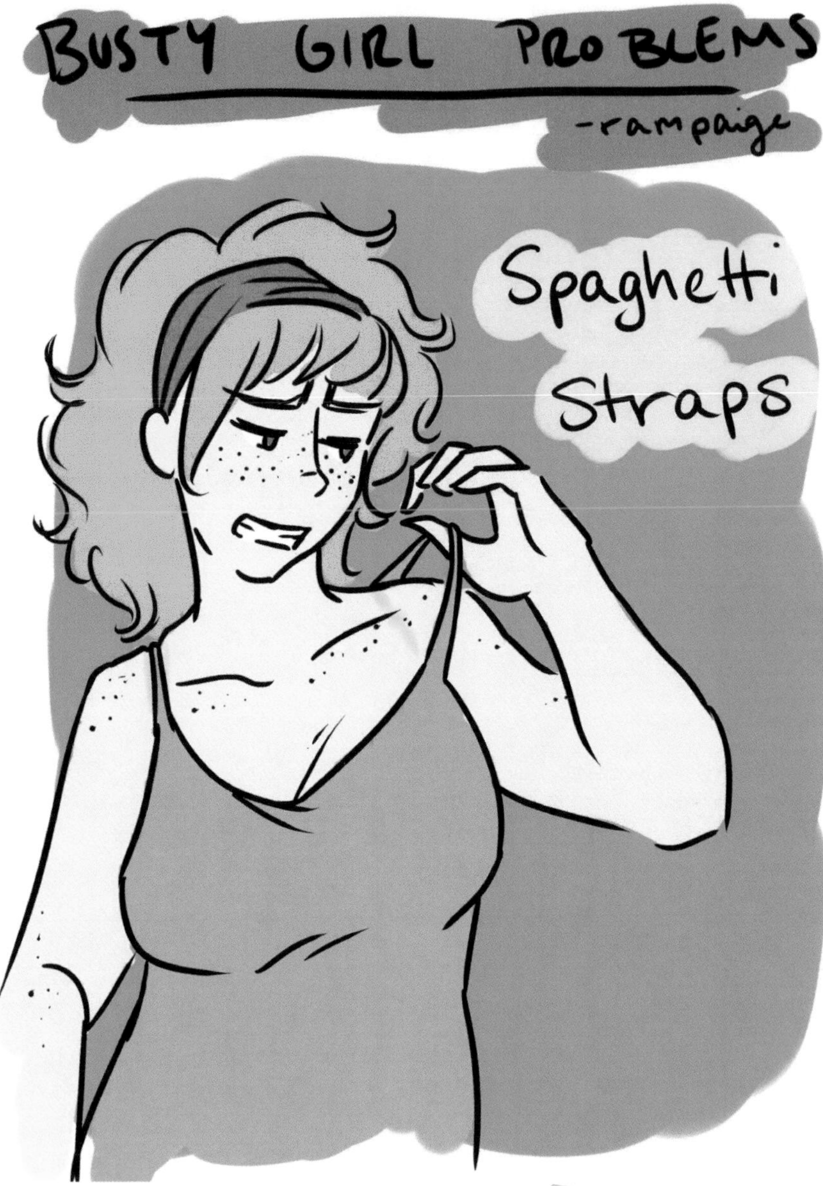
BUSTY GIRL PROBLEMS
-rampaige
Spaghetti Straps

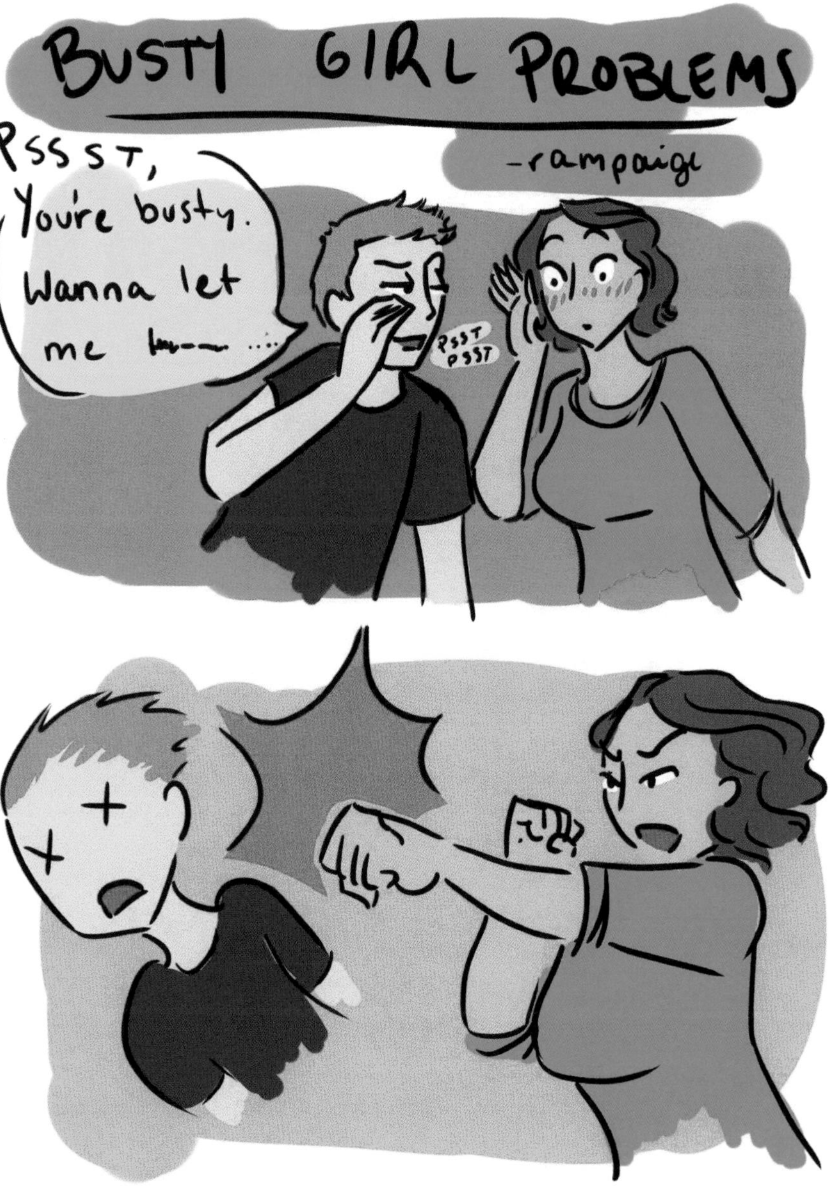
BUSTY GIRL PROBLEMS
-rampaige
Psssst, You're busty. Wanna let me
PSST PSST

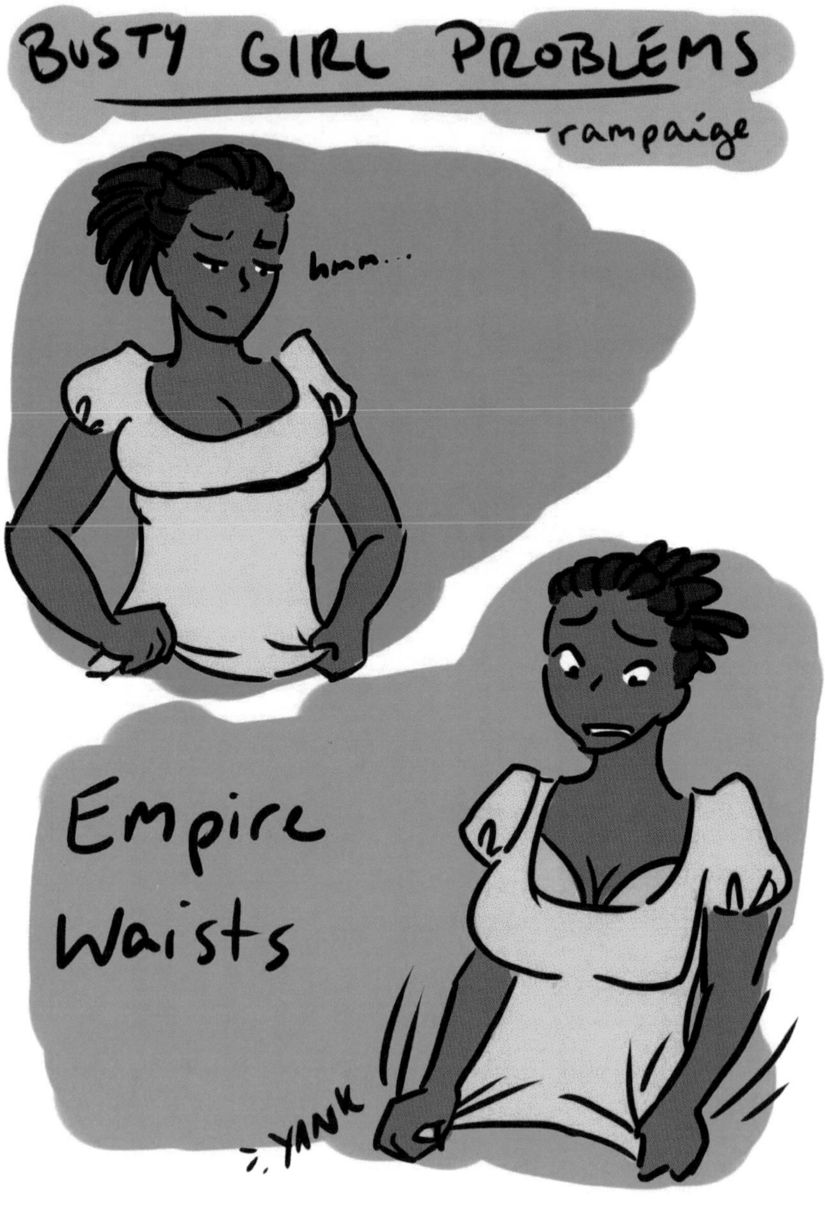
BUSTY GIRL PROBLEMS
-rampaige
hmm...
Empire Waists
YANK

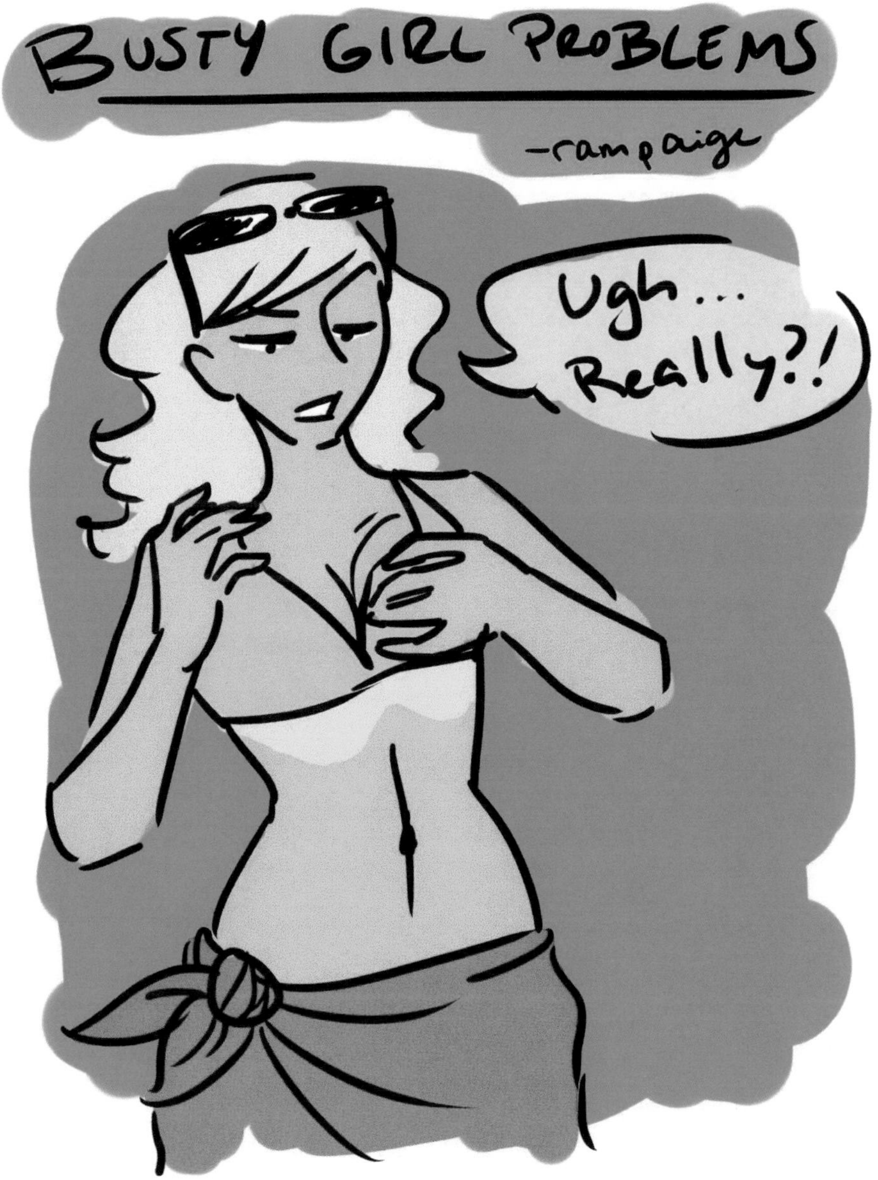
BUSTY GIRL PROBLEMS
-rampaige
Ugh.... Really?!

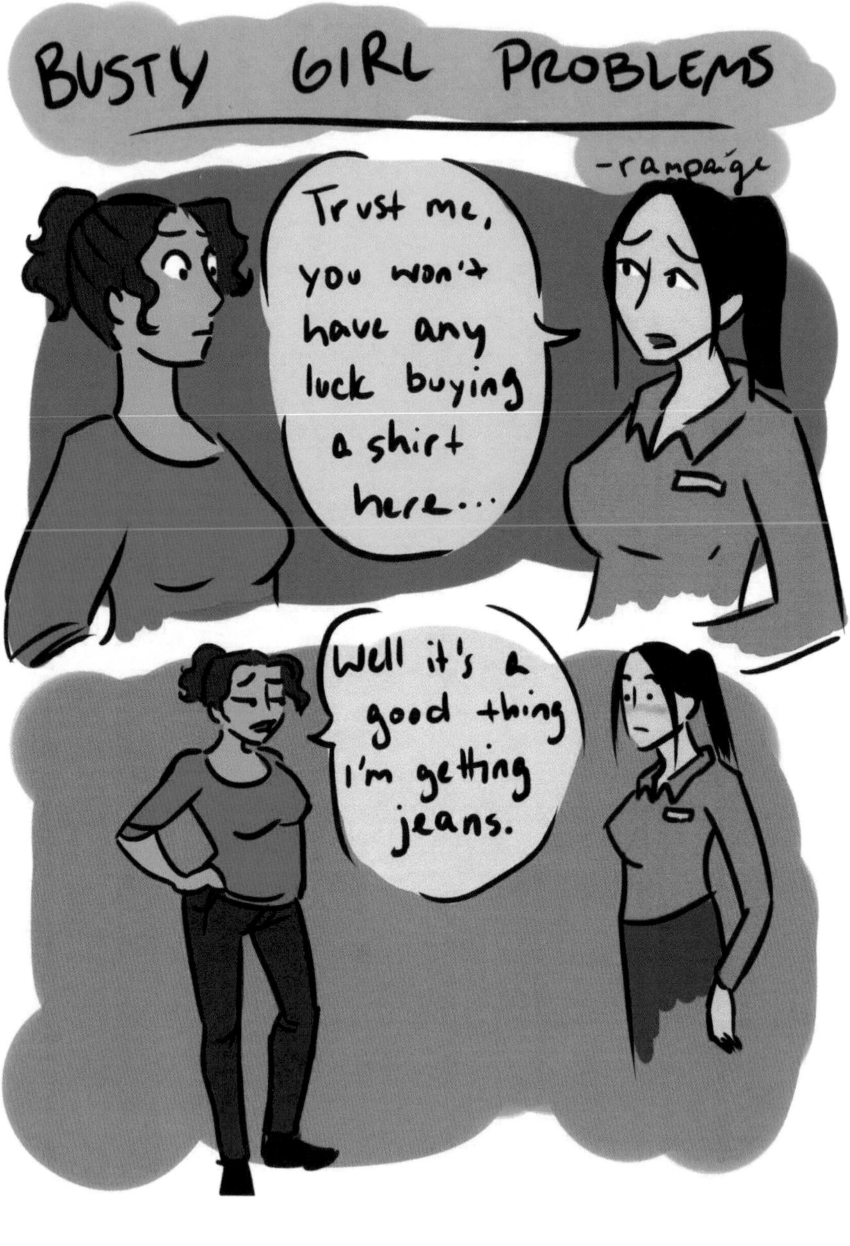
BUSTY GIRL PROBLEMS
-rampaige
Trust me, you won't have any luck buying a shirt here...
Well it's a good thing I'm getting jeans.

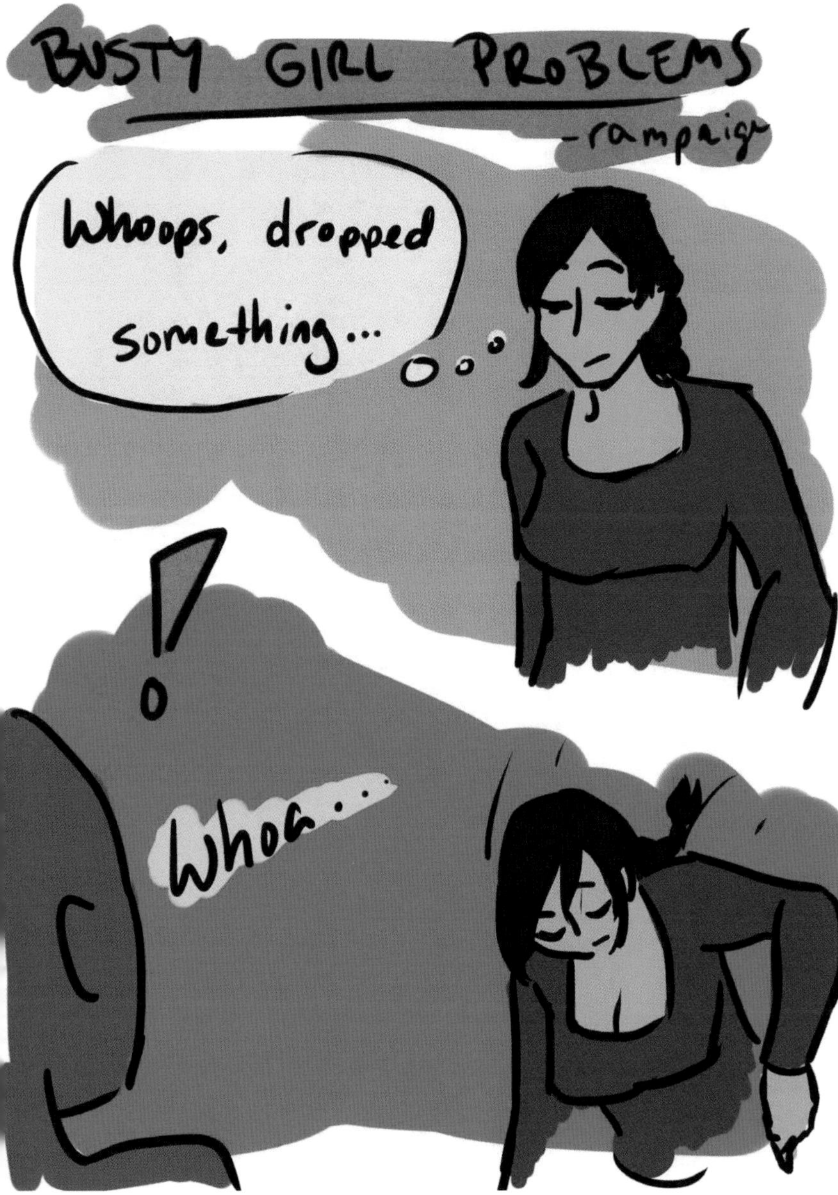
BUSTY GIRL PROBLEMS
-rampaign
Whoops, dropped something...
!
Whoa...

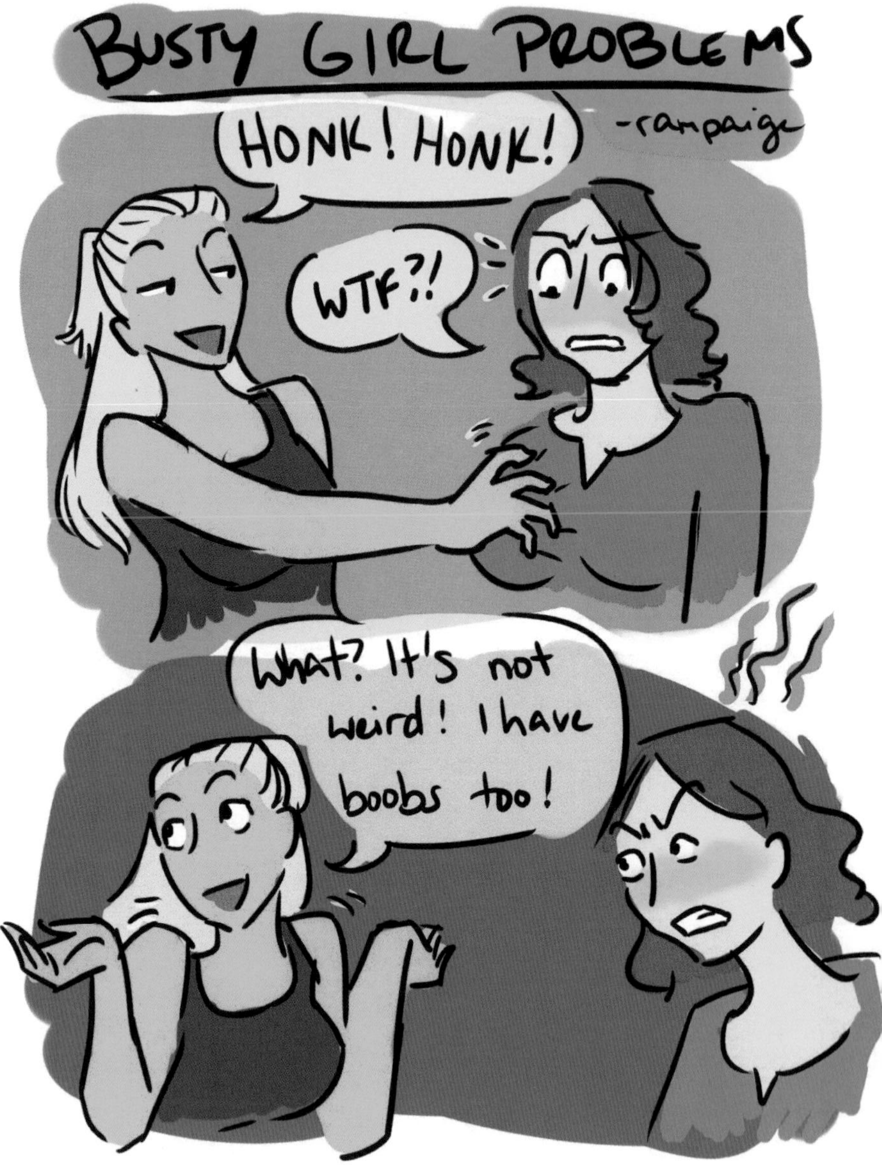
BUSTY GIRL PROBLEMS
-rampaige
HONK! HONK!
WTF?!
What? It's not weird! I have boobs too!

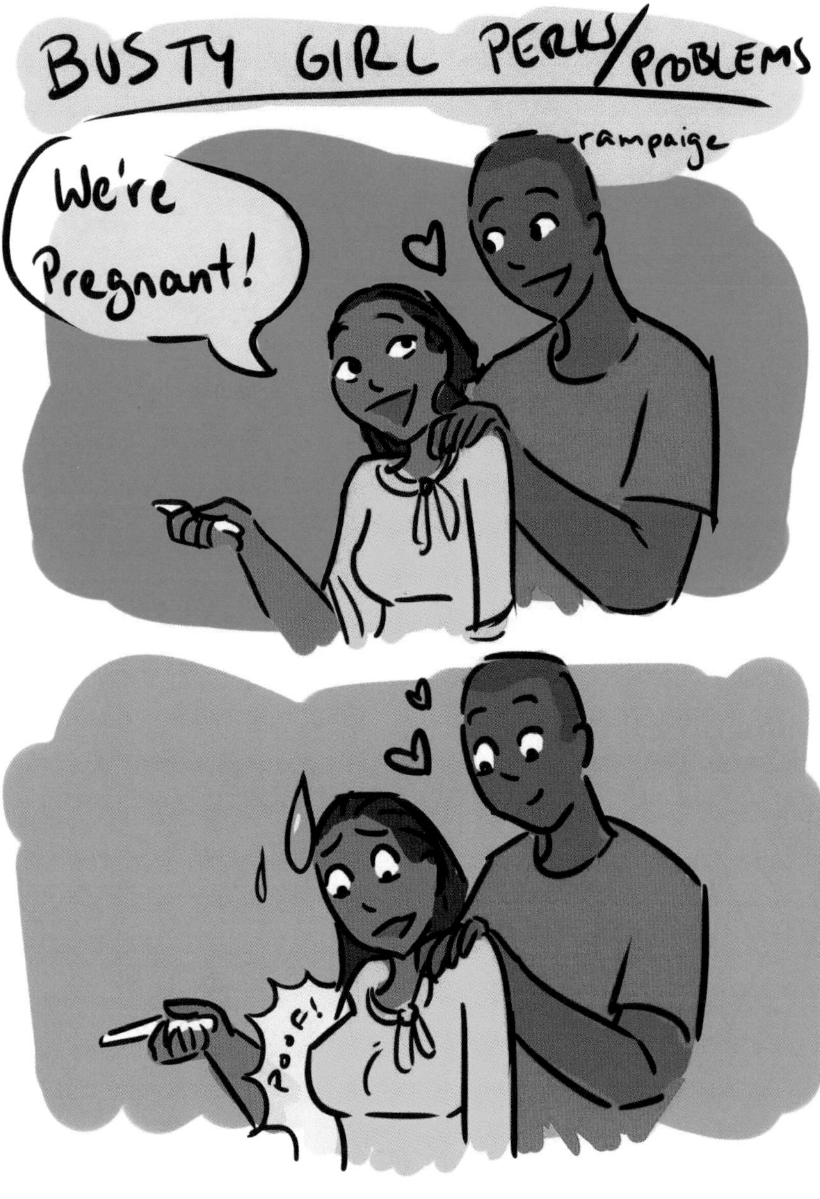
BUSTY GIRL PERKS/PROBLEMS
rampaige
We're Pregnant!
POOF!

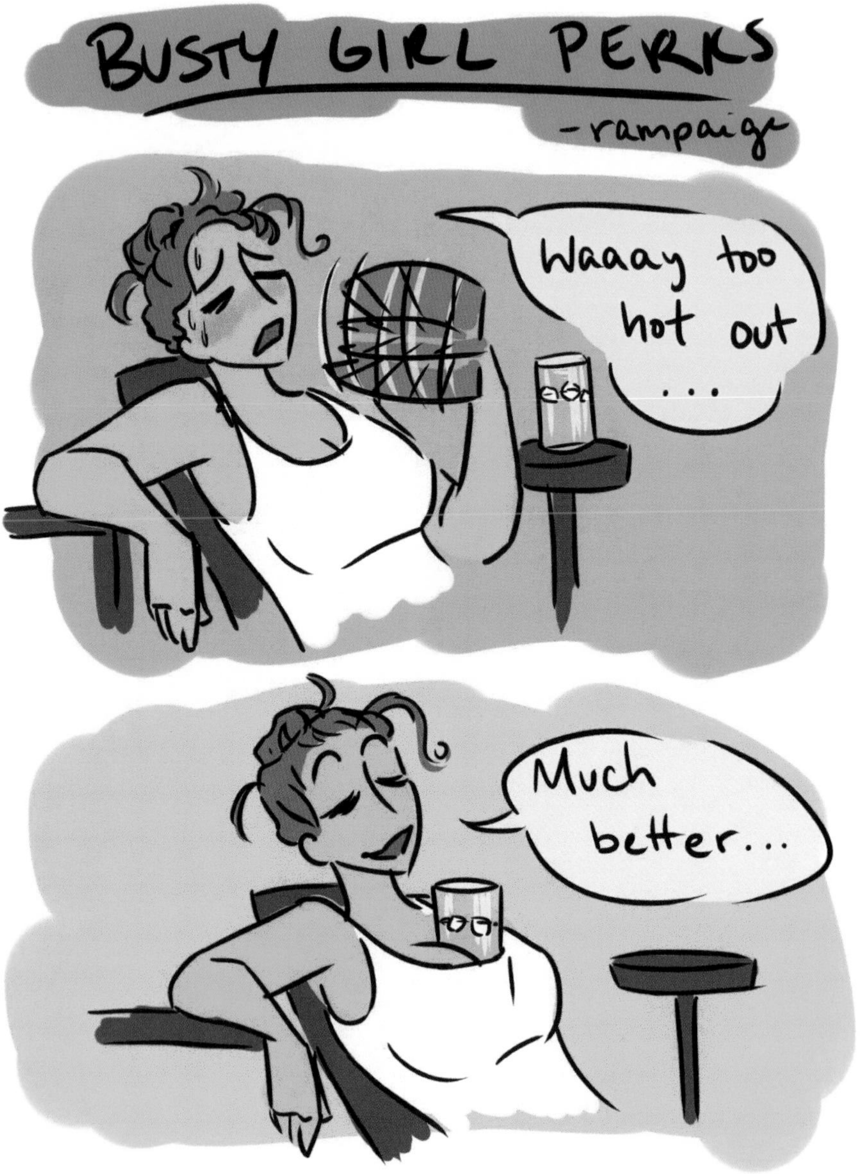
BUSTY GIRL PERKS
-rampaige
Waaay too hot out ...
Much better...

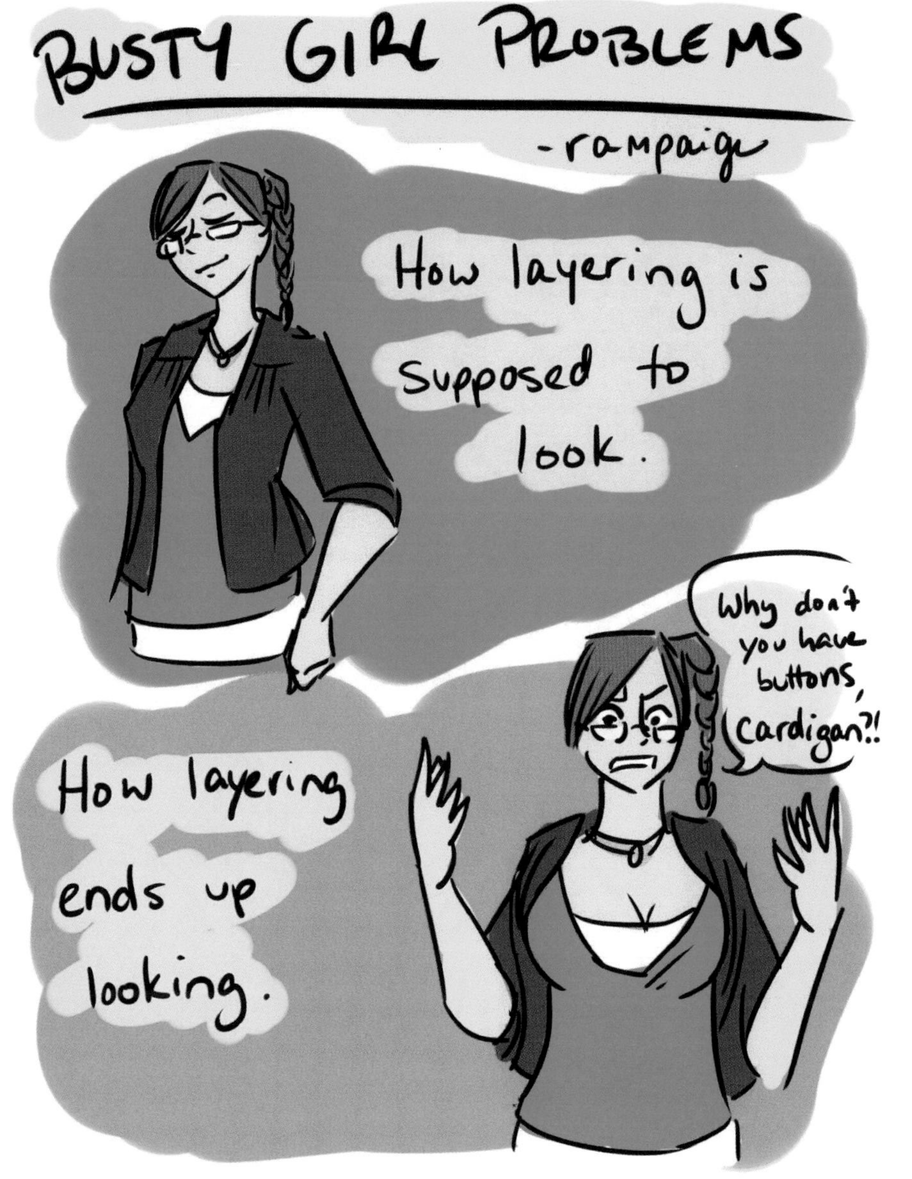
BUSTY GIRL PROBLEMS
-rampaige
How layering is supposed to look.
How layering ends up looking.
Why don't you have buttons, cardigan?!

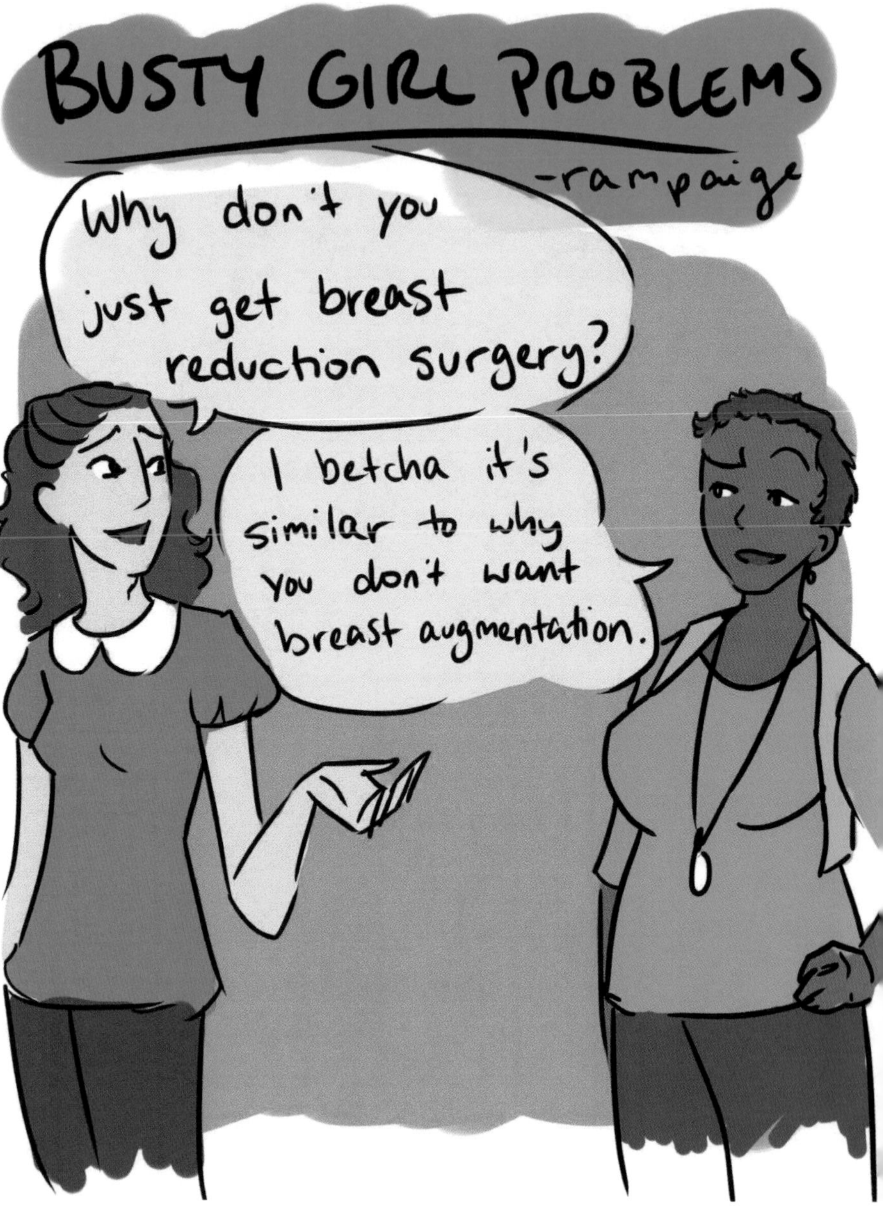
BUSTY GIRL PROBLEMS
-rampaige
Why don't you just get breast reduction surgery?
I betcha it's similar to why you don't want breast augmentation.

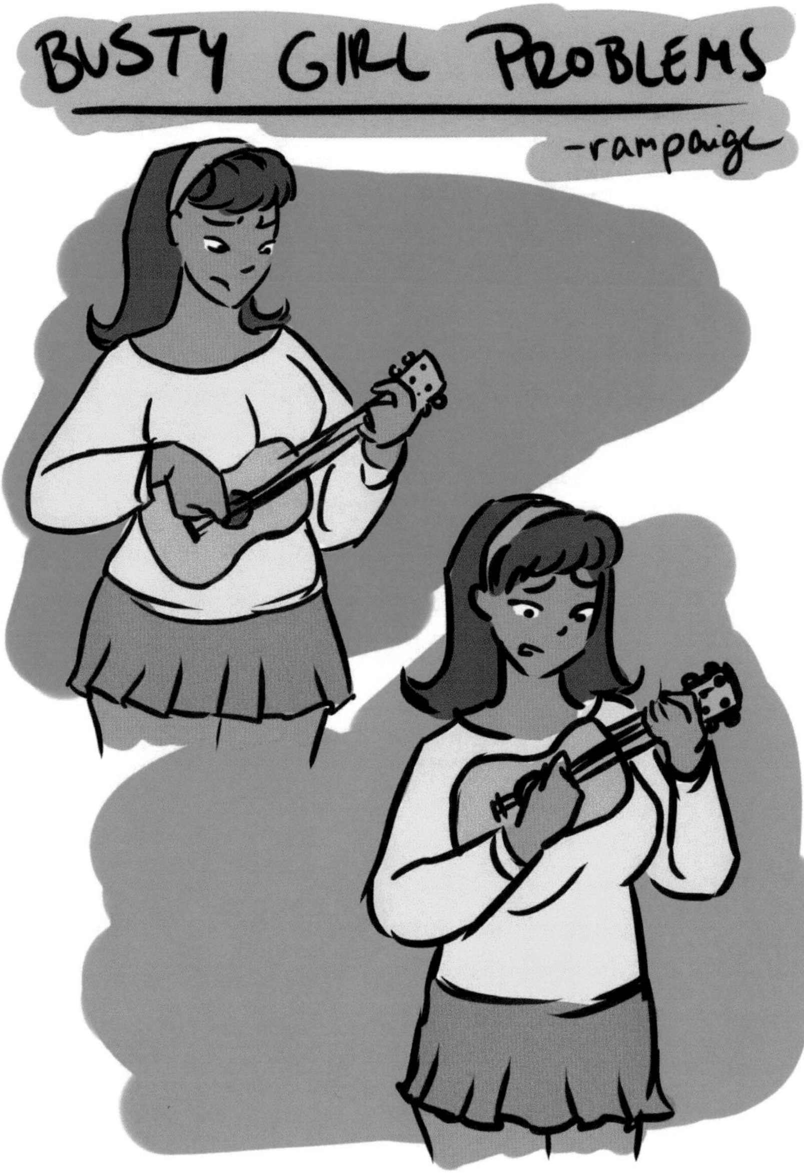
BUSTY GIRL PROBLEMS
-rampaige

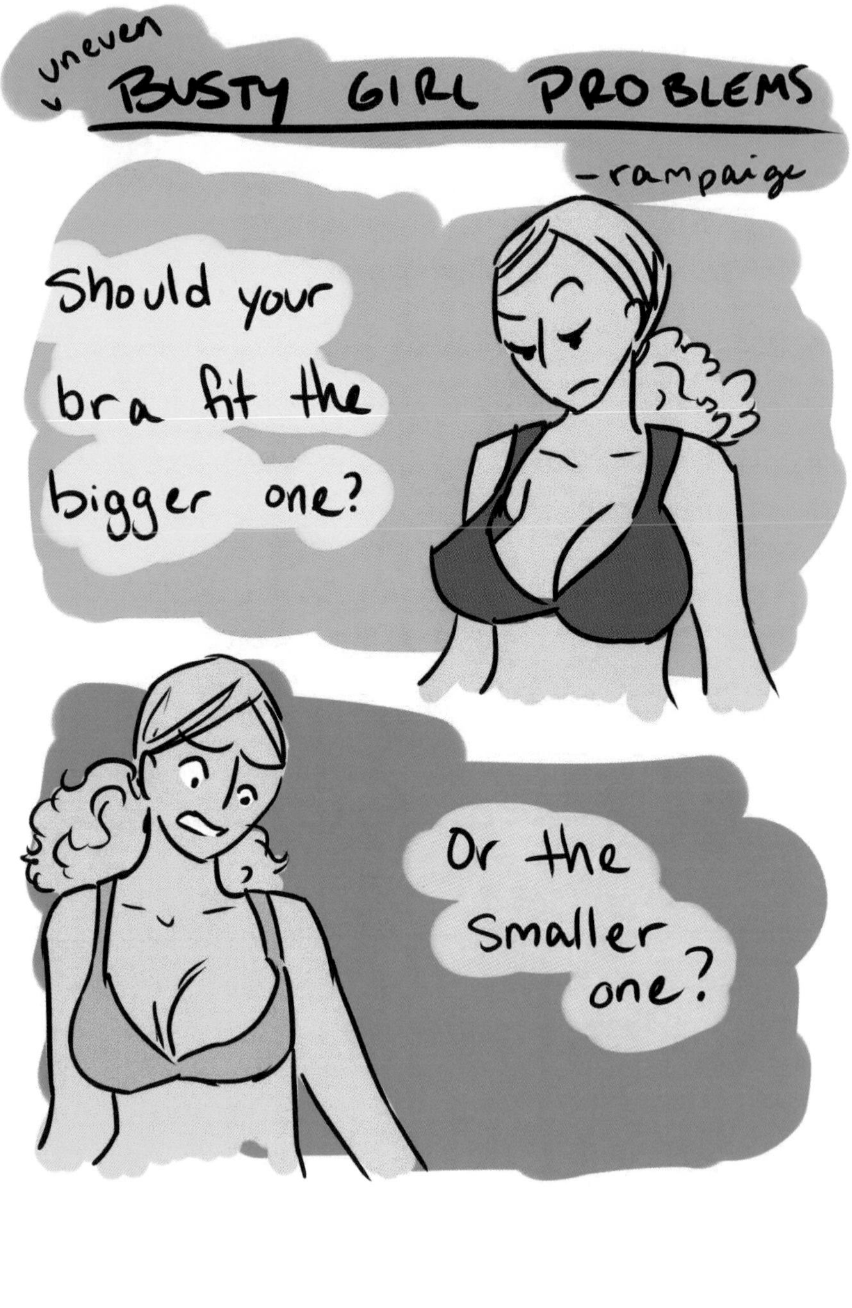
uneven BUSTY GIRL PROBLEMS
-rampaige
Should your bra fit the bigger one?
Or the smaller one?

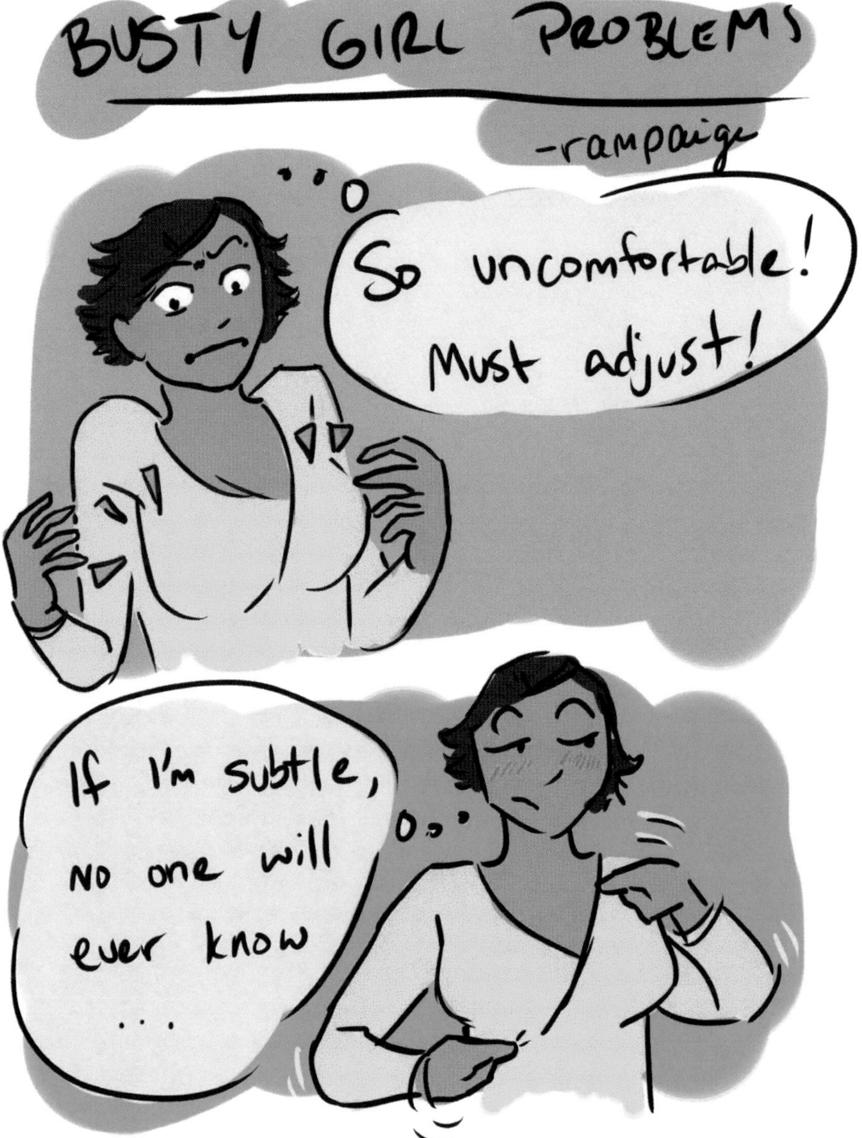
BUSTY GIRL PROBLEMS
-rampaige
So uncomfortable! Must adjust!
If I'm subtle, no one will ever know ...

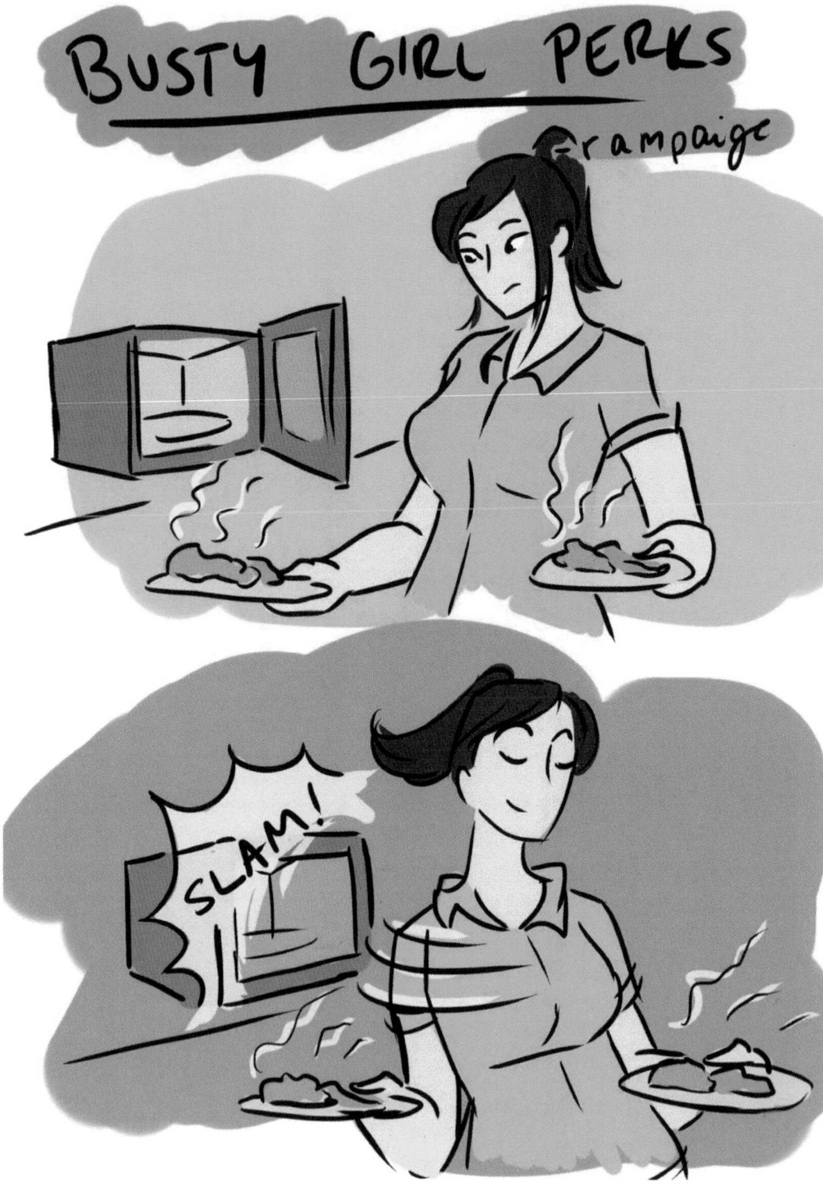
BUSTY GIRL PERKS
@rampaige
SLAM!

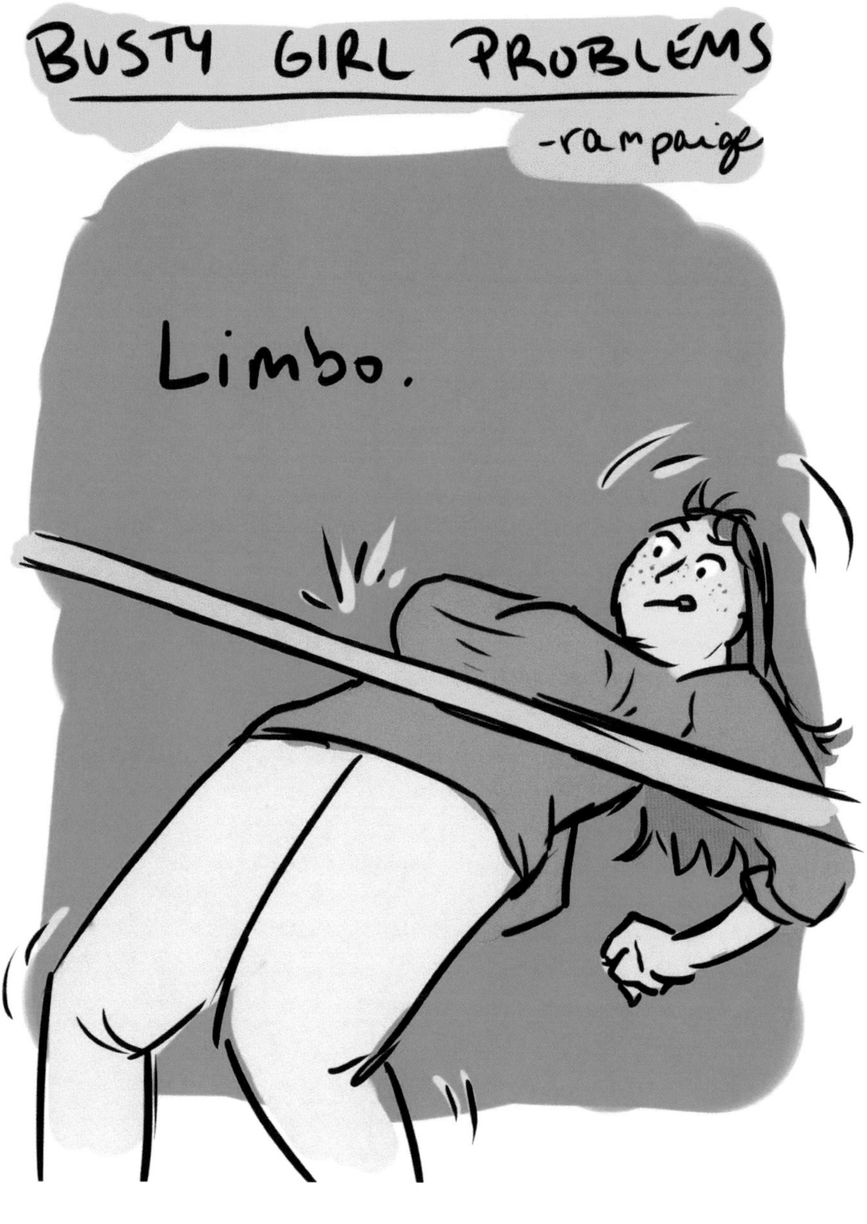
BUSTY GIRL PROBLEMS
-rampaige
Limbo.

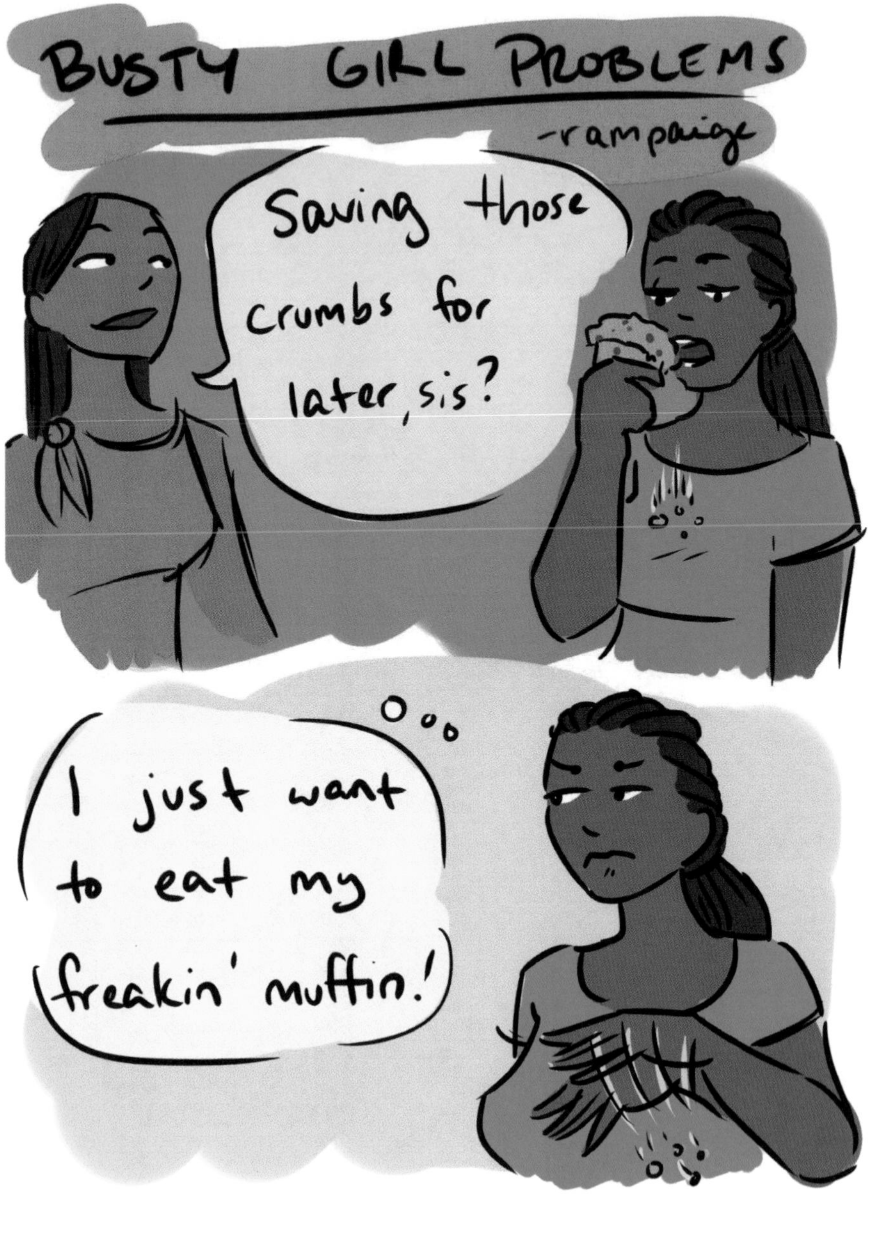
BUSTY GIRL PROBLEMS
-rampaige
Saving those crumbs for later, sis?
I just want to eat my freakin' muffin!

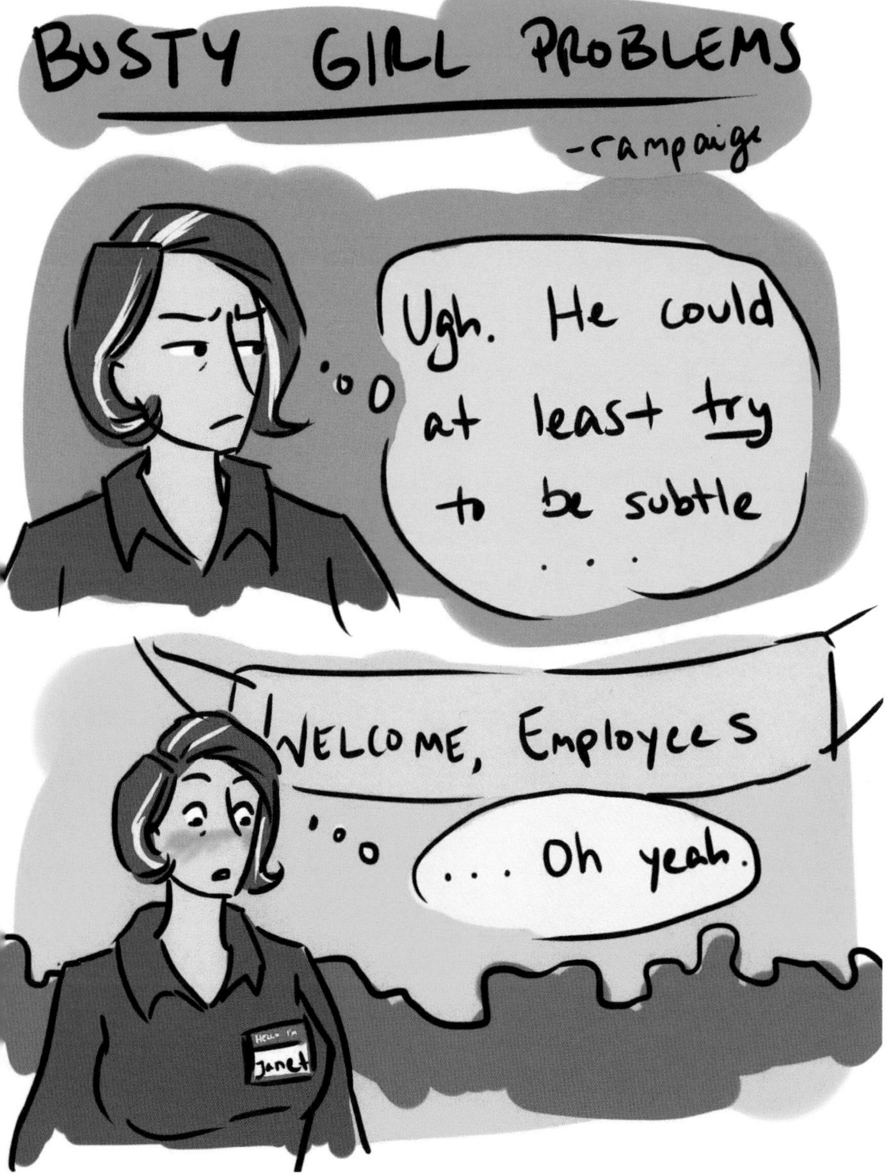
BUSTY GIRL PROBLEMS
-rampaige
Ugh. He could at least try to be subtle . . .
WELCOME, Employees
. . . Oh yeah.
Janet

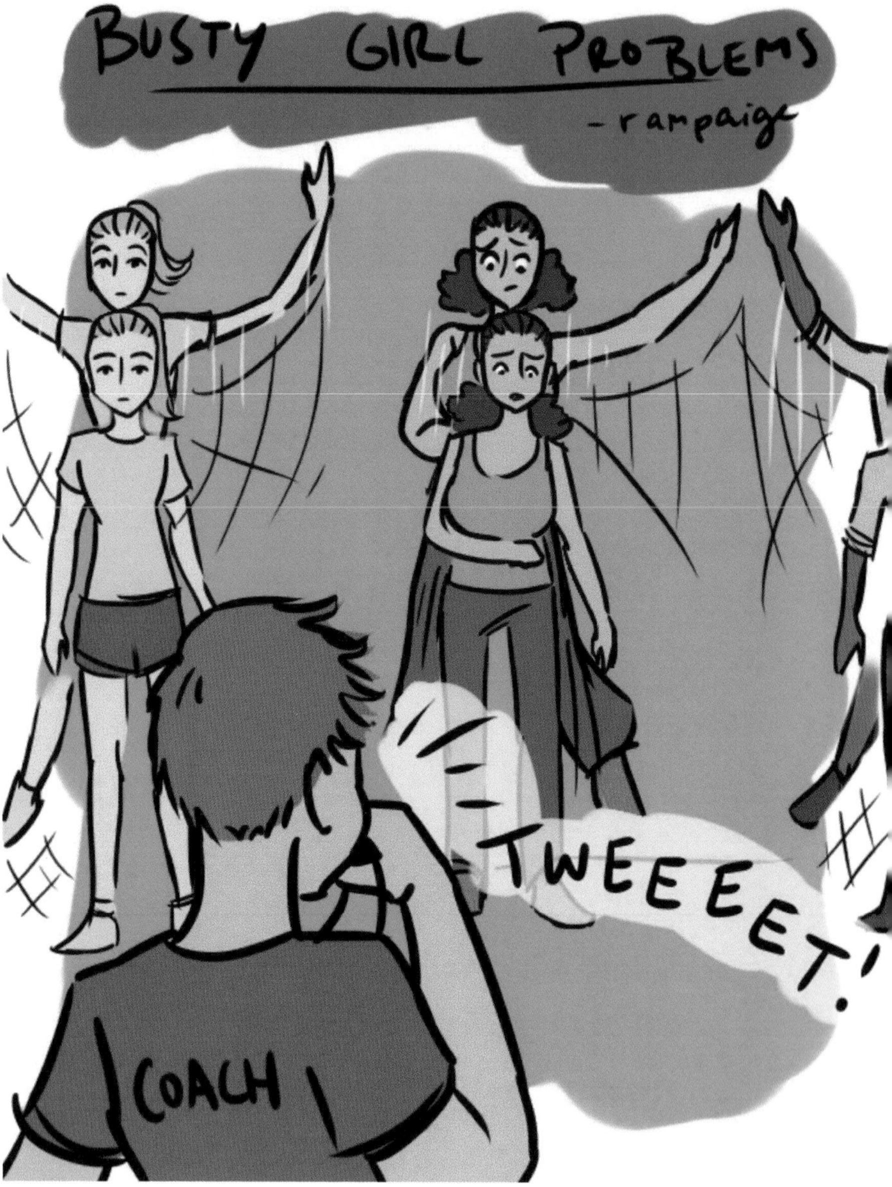
BUSTY GIRL PROBLEMS
-rampaige
TWEEEET!
COACH

Thank you, my wonderful wonderful readers.

I still can't believe that my scribbly little comic has over (at the time of writing this) 29,000 followers on Tumblr, 9,500 likes on Facebook, and 500 followers on Twitter! I mean, seriously!! How epic is that?! Anyway, I just wanted to say thanks to every one of you! You guys came for the lulz and stuck around to help, support, and advise each other. That's pretty freakin' cool!

♡ Rampaige

Rampaige is actually Paige Halsey Warren.
She's really a freelance artist
specializing in character design and
animation but after a frustrating night
of online t-shirt shopping,
Busty Girl Comics was born!

If you want to learn more about
the artist, please check out:
bustygirlcomics.com/rampaige

15294543R00056

Made in the USA
Charleston, SC
27 October 2012